HOW TO WIN PROFITS
AND
INFLUENCE BANKERS

HOW TO WIN PROFITS
AND
INFLUENCE BANKERS

The Art of Practical Projecting

RICHARD C. BELEW

 VAN NOSTRAND REINHOLD COMPANY

New York   Cincinnati   Toronto   London   Melbourne

Van Nostrand Reinhold Company Regional Offices:
New York Cincinnati Chicago Millbrae Dallas

Van Nostrand Reinhold Company International Offices:
London Toronto Melbourne

Copyright © 1973 by Litton Educational Publishing, Inc.

Library of Congress Catalog Card Number: 72-7252
ISBN: 0-442-20665-8

Manufactured in the United States of America

Published by Van Nostrand Reinhold Company
450 West 33rd Street, New York, N.Y. 10001

Published simultaneously in Canada by Van Nostrand Reinhold Ltd.

15 14 13 12 11 10 9 8 7 6 5 4 3 2 1

Library of Congress Cataloging in Publication Data

Belew, Richard C   1928–
   How to win profits and influence bankers.

   1. Accounting. I. Title.
HF5635.B4163   658.1'5   72-7252
ISBN 0-442-20665-8

Introduction

. . . the general run of current self-improvement books shows a rather sharp divergence from the old tradition. On the surface they do not seem to, and their titles promise the old fare. Essentially, however, what they tell you to do is to adjust to the situation rather than change it. . . .

—Page 281, *The Organization Man,*
By WILLIAM H. WHYTE, JR.,
Doubleday Anchor, 1956

HAVING BEEN ATTRACTED BY THE TITLE OF THIS BOOK, PRESUMABLY you have—for one reason or another—some degree of interest in *profits* and/or an interest in being able to influence *bankers*. Whatever the reasons that may make you interested in these subjects, you have the right to know the *intended* purpose of the book—hence this Introduction.

Put briefly, the purposes of this book are threefold:

1. To pass along, to those who can use it, some "know how" having to do with earning profits and influencing bankers, who are often among the key people you must deal with in the course of running a business profitably;

2. To stimulate, especially, some entrepreneur-type people (people who, incidentally, may not read many books!) to do better planning in connection with their business enterprises; and

3. To get this book "out of my system," where it has been like a burr under the saddle for all too long.

Others may enjoy or be able to benefit from reading it, but I may as well confess at the outset that this effort is really aimed (even if obliquely) at a particular kind of audience: men and women who have dreamed of owning or managing a business enterprise of some kind, and who are far enough along with their dreams or efforts to realize that profits are important, and that bankers play a vital role in the affairs of business enterprises, *but* who also realize they can use more "know how" at this particular point in their endeavors. For example, if you are the sales-oriented president of a growing small business, and this book comes your way just as you (with little background in finance) are getting ready to lay out your financial needs for your banker, and you find some useful ideas here—the purpose of this book will have been achieved.

You may not represent the ideal audience at just this time, and still you may find this book to be of interest and value: you could be a student, looking forward to entering the business world; you could be the wife of a man who has been figuring and dreaming about how to get into business for himself for years, and yet doesn't seem to get started in that direction; you could be a banker, curious to know what anyone would have to say about how to influence you; you could be an employee of the Small Business Administration, keen to pick up ways and means of better serving your clientele; or, you might well be an accountant working with entrepreneurs, and be anxious to add to your knowledge in the financial area. Or, finally, you may be the entrepreneur that I'm really aiming at.

Whatever your "situation," we hope to be able to help certain business-oriented people adjust to their "situations" in what will be a personally satisfactory and socially desirable way, and it is hoped that this objective will be achieved with your reading of this book.

Contents

Index of Exhibits

CHAPTER 16

1

How Do You Win Profits?

THE ROLE OF PROFITS

ROFITS ARE USUALLY DEFINED AS THE EXCESS OF RECEIPTS OR INCOME over disbursements or expenditures, either for a single transaction or for a series of transactions. Generally, when profits are referred to in connection with a business, what is meant is "profits after income taxes," which of course means profits after *all* costs, expenses, and taxes of all kinds have been subtracted. This will be the meaning of the term "profits" as discussed in this book.

Although it is not generally touched upon in the definitions that are given for profits, the latter play a very special role in a free-enterprise economy: they provide a yardstick with which to measure economic efficiency. That is, in a rather completely planned economy, such as in Soviet Russia, other standards ("the Agricultural Commission believes 5,000 of these tractors should be manufactured," etc.) may be used to determine whether a factory or service business, or any kind of business enterprise, is functioning properly. In a free-enterprise economy such as we have in the United States, *profits* are the yardstick.

PROFITS AND RIGHTS

Whenever there is a conflict between human rights and property rights, human rights must prevail.

—ABRAHAM LINCOLN

1

Perhaps no facile political slogan has done more mischief in our time than the pretense that there is a conflict between "human rights and property rights": a notion popularized in this country by Franklin Roosevelt. All rights are human rights. Both in point of law and in ethical theory, beasts, plants, and inanimate objects have no rights. Only men and women have rights.

—Page 66, *The Intelligent Woman's Guide to Conservatism,*
By Russell Kirk,
The Devin-Adair Company, New York, 1957.

Profits create property rights, which are transferable into goods and services that can greatly enhance human rights, and for this reason, making money or making profits is really a rather noble goal. Perhaps the most marvelous thing about property rights, which profits create, is that they are convertible into other things. Once one has earned profits, he may utilize them to do a host of things, from buying homes or automobiles to traveling, acquiring further education, investing in other enterprises, or to make charitable contributions. Also, making profits can be fun!

MANAGEMENT BY EXCEPTION

If one had only a paragraph in which to relate the "how" of successful management of business enterprises, it is doubtful if he could choose any one phrase that would be more potent than "management by exception." In other words: *plan,* and then follow up on the plan, *concentrating* on the *exceptions* to the plan. This same approach is sometimes referred to as "management by objectives." It is a well-known, too infrequently used but well-tested and highly recommended procedure—and it is herewith recommended, again, as *the* best approach to the management of business affairs.

"WIN" vs. "EARN"

Profits are often referred to as "earnings," and at first blush you might wonder why you should take issue with the word *earn* as it has to do with profits. At first glance, the above caption might appear to be a mere exercise in semantics; but it is more than that. In fact, far from being merely a matter of literary taste, the author submits that the use of "win" in connection with profits has a practical importance in everyday business life.

"Win" implies a goal, or an objective, and it is *management by objectives* (or, if you will, "management by exception") that you must use in order to successfully manage a business enterprise. Therefore, why not adopt the use of the word *win* in connection with profits? Every day this will remind you that you are "playing a game" and shooting for certain business objectives. It is for a good reason that computer "business games" represent the latest tool in the educational process of the future business managers in the United States.

Another reason for using the word *win* in connection with profits is that to "win" definitely involves competition, or a contest. And certainly the business arena is competitive, if it is anything.

In particular, the author feels that by *using* the word *win* in connection with the word *profits,* one can be *reminded* that the things to concentrate on are the *goals* and *objectives* of the business enterprise. The thing to do is to *lay plans* to meet and overcome the competition, and "let the profits take care of themselves," which they most assuredly will do *if* the goals and objectives are laid out carefully and followed.

It sometimes seems like a paradox, but it is true that often people do find that profits "just come" in some cases, whereas in others they are not to be had despite the fact that someone is striving mightily to achieve them. Why is this? Well, the author believes that it is almost axiomatic that profits are a *by-product* and that one must *first* focus his attention on carrying out the business *objectives*. If this is done properly, the "bottom line" or net profit picture will take care of itself!

2
Why Influence Bankers?

. . . in Great Britain, Canada and the United States the principal form of effective money in circulation for many years has been the demand deposit . . . it is natural for the borrower to take the proceeds of a bank loan in the form of a credit to his deposit balance. An example will serve to emphasize this point. Let us suppose that Mr. John Q. Jones, treasurer of the local retail clothing firm of Jones & Jones, goes to his bank, the City National, to negotiate a seasonal loan in the amount of $5,000. The purpose of this loan is to enable the firm to take cash discounts on invoices of merchandise purchased for the Eastern trade. Mr. Jones tenders to the executive vice-president or to the cashier of the City National Bank his firm's promissory note drawn at 90 days' maturity. The loan is approved by the loan committee of the bank. Does Treasurer Jones want cash? . . . Not at all! What Jones wants is a credit to his firm's deposit balance, against which checks may be drawn to the order of the several suppliers whose invoices Jones wants to pay promptly. . . . Having . . . received the proceeds of the loan as a credit to the firm's deposit balance, Mr. Jones can return to his office and start writing checks. He is as well off as though he had received cash—actually, he is better off . . . .

—Pages 12, 86 and 87,
Money and Banking, Jay L. O'Hara,
Pitman Publishing Corporation, 1948

4

MEN, MONEY, AND MACHINES

MEN, MONEY, AND MACHINES HAVE BEEN DESCRIBED AS THE three vital ingredients to business enterprise. Others like to describe it a different way and say that it is People, Paper, and Processes. Any way you look at it, money is *one* of the vital business resources required to carry on business enterprise.

Banks create money, and in the process make loans to business enterprises. For this reason, it is important, if you are going to manage a business enterprise, to be able to influence bankers; it's really that simple.

A PLANNED ECONOMY

> . . . *the idea of a planned economy was developed and applied in constantly increasing degree. A government planning agency (Gosplan) was formed; its purpose was to plan and co-ordinate the expansion of mining, industry, transportation, and agricultural production throughout the USSR, in accordance with the potentialities and needs of each region. . . . Soviet writers also credit the system of economic planning with the material and psychological preparedness of the country to resist the German attack, to recover from initial enemy successes, and finally to drive out the invaders. Economic planning has also proved its worth in the reconstruction of reoccupied areas, and it will undoubtedly guide the expansion eastward of Soviet industry and agriculture; this is already well advanced and was stimulated during the years of war. The basis of Soviet planned economy is the immense and still largely undeveloped natural resources of the country. Industry, accordingly, is continuously projected into the future, as these resources are uncovered, charted, evaluated, and, when promising, developed.*

> —Pages 256 and 257 from Chapter XIII,
> "Industry Under the Soviet Government"
> by ERNEST C. ROPES, in the book
> *USSR: A Concise Handbook,*
> edited by Ernest J. Simmons,
> Cornell University Press, 1947.

Think, for a moment, of the difference in the manner in which resources are allocated in the Soviet Union and in the United States. Any intelligent appraisal of the progress made by Russia will leave one impressed with what they have been able to do with all of their economic planning. Nevertheless, in recent years they have adopted some of the features of a profit system, where it fits in with their plans. However, an individual who would be called an entrepreneur in the United States would not, in Soviet Russia, have an opportunity to develop his own idea into a business in the manner in which people are able to do it regularly here.

In a sense, here in the United States one can "start from the top," and work down. That is, one can go to the bank and discuss with the banker one's program. If he is able to win support for it, he can go ahead with his business plans. There is no mechanism permitting individuals in the Soviet type of economy to operate in this manner.

Perhaps the whole theme of this book can best be explained at this point: what is needed is *more planning* by individual enterprises in the United States economy. By more planning, what is meant is not some overall, directed, committee-type effort, but instead *better planning by the business managers who are running businesses.*

SELL YOURSELF TO THE BANKER

Although the primary reason that the bank lending officer—or banker as we will refer to him—is so important to you is that he can loan you money for your business, bankers are also useful in other respects. Often bankers act as catalysts in different situations: they bring together buyers and sellers, they introduce competitors to each other, they pass along ideas that they encounter in the course of their work, and they are good advisers as to the economic picture.

Bankers will understand what you mean when (and *if*) you can show them that you run your business on the principle of "management by exception," and they can help you, in a host of ways, to "win" profits.

There are over 14,000 banks in the United States, and many of these have a number of branches; so another reason for trying to get in a position where you can influence your banker is the fact that he is *handy,* and can be useful to you because he is there, holding out his bank to be of service to people as his prime business function.

The banker has much to do with the development of your business image. That is, other people will see you through the eyes of the banker, in a number of instances. For example, when you seek credit from trade suppliers or other parts of the business community, those people will be contacting your banker to get a credit reference. Therefore, what your banker thinks of you and your business becomes vitally important even if you never need to call on him for a loan.

Having touched lightly on the complex matter of banking, it probably next makes sense to talk a little bit about the matter of borrowing money from a bank or other type of financial institution.

3
Borrowing

The rich ruleth over the poor, and the borrower is servant to the lender.

—Proverbs 22:7

BORROWING IS A SERIOUS BUSINESS. IT SHOULD NOT BE UNDERtaken lightly. In the past, too much borrowing has been done on the basis of the borrower seeking an amount of money which represents only a guess on his part as to his needs, and a lender granting less than what the borrower asks, simply on the principle that "it is good to be conservative."

There are still too many instances where the borrower is so uninformed himself that he is not able to make an intelligent presentation to the lender, and the lender is, in the end, also relatively ignorant of the factors involved in the loan, so that he is bound to "take the conservative route." In doing so, he may possibly make the classical error of not being able to supply enough money to do the job.

TYPES OF BORROWING

There are various ways of classifying loans. They may be typed as secured or unsecured, and as short-term or long-term. (They could also be classified as "good" loans and "bad" loans!) What is important is that the borrower as well as the lender understands exactly what type of borrowing is involved. Attention to this basic, fundamental premise would correct and prevent many confused situations in the lending world.

A classification according to how the money is to be *repaid* might be the most meaningful designation of loans. It has been said that there are only three ways in which money can be repaid:

1. From the sale of an asset;
2. From profits or other increases in net worth, such as from a sale of stock; and
3. To get another lender; "borrow from Peter to pay Paul."

Sometimes a bank loan "turns sour" because a lending officer thought it represented a seasonal-type loan (which would be repaid from the sale of assets, or the movements of inventories or accounts receivable) when, in reality, the loan could never have been repaid on that basis, but had to be repaid from profits. In such a case, the banker winds up with a relatively *long*-term loan when he was expecting a *short*-term one.

The traditional story of bank lending has to do with a toy merchant who borrows from the bank to build up his inventory in September, October, and November, and makes big sales in December. He uses the money that he borrowed from the bank to pay for the toy inventory, and the movement out, in terms of sales of the toy inventory, provides the money with which to repay the loan. Note that in such a case it is *not* necessary that the toy merchant make a *profit* on his sales; the simple movement of goods through his business will provide the funds with which to repay the loan. This is the traditional and classic example of the first type of loan mentioned above.

There are several examples that would serve, but one that perhaps serves best is the example of an equipment loan for situation "2" described above. Here both borrower and lender can expect profits to pay for a loan, and the equipment that is being purchased must be a profitable addition to the business. In particular, the borrower should be able to show the banker how he can repay the loan over a period of, say, thirty-six months. This repayment will come about as the result of profits earned by new machinery and equipment, used in conjunction with other business assets.

The third type of borrowing mentioned above (where you simply get another lender to take out the first one) is generally not too constructive. It often represents a failure in communication and in the design and carrying out of a loan program. For example, a borrower who approached one bank for what he thought was a short-term loan, but which really turned out to be a term credit which should have run over at least four years, might well have "encountered trouble" at his bank, and might have to have moved to another bank. The second bank might (properly) have analyzed the situation as having been the result of a *mistaken* need being filled with the *wrong* type of credit, and taken on the borrower on his *long-term* credit basis, rather than for short-term credit.

Another intelligent way to look at borrowing is to ask "Why?"

WHY BORROW?

The question above can perhaps be answered briefly by saying that you should only borrow money when you need to. Or, that you should only borrow money when it proves, on analysis, to be profitable for you to do so.

Another concept that enters the picture is that of "Return on Investment." To illustrate this, suppose that a company had a net worth of $100,000 at the beginning of a particular business year. Let us further suppose that it badly needed to borrow $50,000, and that it thought it could borrow this money at 8%. That would amount to interest payments of $4,000 a year. The rate of 8% sounded high to the borrower, at first, but then, on reflection, he realized that he expected to *earn* $35,000 after all taxes and interest, *provided* that he could borrow the $50,000. This means that his return on investment would be 35% ($35 thousand related to $100 thousand), compared to the 8% that he was paying for his money, so obviously it made sense for him to borrow the money.

WHERE TO BORROW

Since it is neither necessary nor desirable that the owners of a business invest sufficient funds to take care of all variable working capital needs, such funds may be obtained through short-term loans. The primary source of such current capital for most business is still the commercial bank even though in some situations commercial credit (finance) companies, factors, and suppliers of merchandise may extend a substantial amount of credit.

—Page 297, *Business Finance,*
by CARL A. DAUTEN,
Prentice-Hall, Inc., 1948

Depending on the nature of the need, the logical place to borrow the money that a business needs may be a commercial bank, a commercial credit or finance company, the Small Business Administration, individuals, or small business investment companies, better known as SBICs. This list, however, overlooks perhaps the *easiest* place to obtain credit: from your trade creditors. Trends and statistics in recent years indicate that more and more trade creditors are supplying credit by liberalizing terms to their customers. Much of this is done in a very *un*systematic manner, but we are thinking here of the type of trade credit that can be obtained in a planned way from a manufacturer or supplier, *if* they are provided with a program that indicates it obviously makes sense for them to extend credit on more than the usual terms.

HOW TO BORROW

What you should take with you when you talk to your banker (or other lender) about a loan will vary. In one case, perhaps the only thing you would take is your most recent financial statement. In another case, you may need to take in an elaborate projection of your financial affairs, showing what your seasonal need is and what your long-term need is. It is the purpose of this book to help you in the latter type situation.

In one case you may have done a lot of figuring of ratios yourself in advance of the interview, and, recognizing that one picture can be worth many words, you may have drawn a couple of charts, or taken a picture of part of your factory to bring along with you. If you are talking about a secured loan, you may have a particular exhibit with you that shows the amount of collateral available at any particular time as against the loan need. If you are a growing company, and you have just drawn up your first organizational chart, that might be an exhibit that you would take with you for the loan presentation. If your problem has been to achieve sales beyond a break-even point, you may have a break-even chart as an exhibit. The essential element is that you *"know what you are talking about"* when you go in and talk to the banker, or whoever else may be the lender.

Good communication in business affairs is not possible without some familiarity with the *language of accounting*. Put yourself "in the other guy's shoes." In other words, suppose *you* are a banker. Don't you have to understand accounting in order to read, meaningfully, the financial statements that are presented to you? And, shouldn't you, as a borrower, be at least as well informed as the lender?

Which leads to the next chapter . . .

4

The Language Is Accounting

Now, if you forget everything else I've told you, please *remember this: look at me now, and remember that I have one hand in each pocket; a left hand pocket and a right hand pocket; now, the* left *hand pocket is for DEBITS, and the* right *hand pocket is for CREDITS; now, all you must remember is that you must always put equal amounts in each pocket—that is, the debits must always equal the credits; remember, also, that debits are for what is, in some sense, "coming in" to the business, and that credits are for what is, in some sense or other, "going out." Now—you should understand double entry bookkeeping.*

—VIRGIL APP, about 1944

IT IS NECESSARY TO ASSUME SOME KNOWLEDGE OF ACCOUNTING IN A book like this. But at the same time, we do not wish to assume too much; often a business manager will have been brought up without too much exposure to accounting, and will never have been comfortable with the subject. This is unfortunate and really crippling for anyone involved in business, because in business the language *is* accounting.

There are numerous good books in the "Business" section of the local public library which can supply whatever degree of information one seeks about the theory and practice of accounting. What is going to be attempted here is something that will *not* be as good as a trip to the library, but which may still serve some purpose, for some particular readers. There are, with accounting, certain fundamentals, just as with any other subject.

DOUBLE ENTRY BOOKKEEPING

Just as the term implies, with double entry bookkeeping *two* entries are made for each transaction. Entries are always made to certain particular accounts. There are various types of accounts in any accounting system.

A CHART OF ACCOUNTS

In every accounting system, either you already have a chart of accounts drawn up, or it is easy to draw one up. All that is involved is simply *listing* all of the accounts that you have in your ledger. The usual order brings certain kinds of accounts first, certain other accounts second, etc.

Asset Accounts

Asset accounts, representing things that are owned, carry the names of such assets as "Cash," "Accounts Receivable," "Inventory," "Machinery and Equipment," etc. These accounts might be numbered, with the first asset account carrying the number "101," etc. Asset accounts normally have *debit* balances. This is because you *debit* an asset when it "comes into" the business.

Liability Accounts

This group consists of such items as "Notes Payable," "Accounts Payable," "Accrued Liabilities," "Contracts Payable," etc. Liabilities are what is owed to others, and any kind of account that has that meaning is a liability account. This group of accounts might be numbered "201," "202," etc. Liability accounts normally have *credit* balances. This is because you *credit* an account when your promise to pay "goes out" of the business.

Net Worth Accounts

Net worth accounts include, if you are a corporation, such items as "Common Stock," "Capital Surplus," and "Retained Earnings." (If your business is not incorporated you may simply have one account, "Net Worth," or two accounts, if there are two partners.) The reason that these accounts are of special importance to the owner of the business is that they reflect what belongs to the business, or to its owner, *after* all of the liabilities have been paid. Assets minus liabilities equal net worth. If you are successful in winning profits, these go into your net worth section and increase the size of your worth; if you lose money, it subtracts from your net worth.

Net worth accounts, like liability accounts, normally have a credit balance. This is because what normally happens, as you earn profits, is that the business "promises to pay" *you,* the owner.

If you do not already possess a chart of accounts for your accounting system, this is a good time to stop and obtain or prepare one. You should become familiar with the chart; it will simplify your communication with accounting people.

Income Accounts

Another group in the chart consists of income accounts, the principal one of which is "Sales." In a particular business there may be other income accounts, but in some cases this will be the only one. Clearly, entries are made to sales accounts when sales are made. Income accounts normally have *credit* balances. This is because it is sales that "move the goods out" of the business.

Cost and Expense Accounts

Cost accounts are a group of accounts which record the cost of sales. In a particular business, the nature of these will vary, but in the case of a grocery store, for example, there would be an account to represent the cost of the groceries, with one account for canned goods, a separate one for meats, etc.

Expenses are likewise grouped in a separate category, and if assets were a "100" series of accounts, liabilities "200," net worth accounts "300," income accounts "400," then costs would probably be "500" and expense accounts would be numbered "600," etc. Some orderly system of identification is necessary, and that is the general pattern that is used. Both cost and expense accounts normally have *debit* balances. (Because costs and expenses "come into" the business.)

Now, with an actual chart of accounts for your own accounting system in front of you, or at least some conception of what such a list might look like for an accounting system, it may be well to make a few simple entries, to get the idea of how these accounts are used.

TYPICAL ENTRIES

In some form or other, when sales are made on a credit basis, an account called "Accounts Receivable" will be debited and an account entitled "Sales" will be credited. In the vernacular of Mr. App (see quotation above), what "came in" was the promise of someone to pay you for the goods (or an Account Receivable) and what "went out" was the goods (or an account to keep track of the goods sold, called Sales).

In a similar vein, let us suppose that you buy merchandise. In some fashion, the entry will probably be a debit to an account called "Purchases," in the Cost section of the chart of accounts, and the credit will be to "Accounts Payable," a liability account. What "came in" was the merchandise purchased, and what "went out" was a promise to pay, or an Account Payable.

Once you become accustomed to asking questions about accounting matters in terms of entries, with reference to the chart of accounts, a lot of the mystery of accounting goes out the window.

FINANCIAL STATEMENTS

There are two principal statements that are drawn up periodically to recapitulate or summarize all the entries that have been made in your accounting system. The first of these is known as a Balance Sheet (balancing assets against liabilities and net worth) and the second is known as a Profit and Loss Statement (showing whether you have made a profit or a loss in your operation).

Balance Sheets

A balance sheet summarizes three types of accounts: *asset* accounts, *liability,* accounts and *net worth* accounts. For this reason, these three types of accounts are called "balance sheet accounts." Assets represent things that are owned, liabilities things that are owed, and the net worth is what is owed to the owners of the business, or what is left over after the liabilities are subtracted from the assets.

A balance sheet, it has been said, is like a photograph or a snapshot; it shows the status of accounts as of the close of business on a particular day. Things could change drastically immediately after, or they might have appeared in a completely different way immediately prior to the balance sheet date. For this reason, it has become customary to prepare balance sheets at regular intervals, such as at the end of each month. Some businesses prepare a balance sheet only as of the end of the year, but this frequency is inadequate.

Profit and Loss Statements

Profit and loss statements cover the *income, cost,* and *expense* categories of accounts. The function of a P. and L. statement is to describe what happened during a particular *period* of time, such as for a month or a year.

Another way to think of this is to think of the P. and L. as describing everything that happened "between snapshots." That is, for example, suppose you have in your left hand a balance sheet for December 31 a year ago, and in your right hand a balance sheet for December 31 of the next year. One year will have elapsed between the two statements, and it is the function of the profit and loss statement to explain *what* has happened *between* these two dates, in terms of operations. In other words, a P. and L. summarizes all of the entries that have been made during this time to the income, cost, and expense accounts.

Now: how can we *use* "the language of accounting"? Can it help us plan or project?

5

Where Have We Been?

After a two year investigation of business failures, the University of Pittsburgh's Bureau of Business Research reports that many of them failed because they relied on a constant economic updraft to maintain earnings and solvency, instead of diagnosing and correcting their own operational weaknesses. The study lists 9 fair weather hazards:

1. Slipshod accounting.

2. Failure to diversify.

3. Investing too much in fixed assets.

4. Too many relatives on the payroll.

5. False confidence, leading to expansion without regard to market limitations.

6. Extending credit without sufficient checking.

7. Failure to detect and shift with changes in buying habits.

8. Neglecting tax considerations.

9. Lack of an organized sales plan.

—8/1/69 *Creditorial,*
official publication of the
North Central Credit and
Financial Management Association

PREPARING A FINANCIAL PROJECTION WHICH REFLECTS THE PLANS OF A business for a period ahead is a complex matter. Therefore, as with anything else complex, it is best approached by "breaking it down into pieces."

Essentially, the projection process is one of moving from *knowns* to *unknowns.* Thus, the *first* step in the process is to take a good, hard analytical look *backward.* Once we "know where we've been" we can look ahead to the future a little more knowledgeably. The process is somewhat akin to that of a physical examination by a doctor. The first thing the physician must do is to develop a history about you, so he can then diagnose you against this background. And for similar reasons, we will follow a similar course. The "physical examination" that we will give to the business we are studying here (instead of *your own* business figures, which of course are not available at this point) involves *thirty* different steps.

Ten of these steps involve an analysis of various aspects of the *balance sheet;*

twenty of the tests deal with the *profit and loss statement*. *Please* try to accept "automatic revulsion" at having to look at so many facts and figures: you should be just as curious to find out what an analysis of this business brings to light as you would be about the results of tests given to you at a medical clinic. In any event, each "test" will be treated and discussed individually—and as briefly as makes sense.

BALANCE SHEET SPREAD

If you have ever submitted financial statements to a bank or other lender, you may have wondered what they *do* with them—other than to "read and study" them. Well, one of the standard procedures involves "spreading" your statements—which means, simply, that the various statements are set *side by side,* in an orderly manner, with one item on one line, so that they may be viewed in a way that makes changes and trends "stand out." Look at Exhibit 1 and you will see what five consecutive balance sheets look like when "spread" for the business we will be studying. . . . See anything interesting? What do *you* think would catch the eye of a sharp banker, as he scanned this section of his credit file on this company?

Without being exhaustive, here—in a "stream of consciousness" fashion—are at least some of the thoughts that might well have occurred to the banker as he looked at the Exhibit. Compare these with your own thoughts:

Cash: When did this company begin banking here? It looks like they used to have overdrafts, but their cash balances look better in recent years; I should get out our account card and see what it shows about how profitable this account has been to our bank (OR—would this account be profitable, if we took it away from the First National Bank?)

Accounts Receivable: I would like to look at an aging of these accounts, to see how many are old, and if there is any concentration in the receivables; also, I wonder what their terms of sale are. . . .

Finished Goods Inventory: I've never really had an opportunity to examine closely one of the "widgets" that this company makes—suppose I will be able to do this when I go out there. Anyway, these finished goods should be good collateral: the "widgets" are popular, and we have financed some for dealers on the retail level, with—I believe (better check on this!)—a repurchase agreement from *this* company, to support our loan.

Raw Materials Inventory: They must use a lot of steel in this product, so the raw steel would be fair collateral. . . . I wonder if they buy from Ajax Steel; my neighbor, Ted Smith, could probably tell me about this—he's been with Ajax a long time, and would probably know how these people are regarded in the trade.

Claim—Income Taxes: This must mean that they lost some money in year 3; anyway, I should remember to ask to see copies of their tax returns, and to find out when they were last examined, cleared.

Fixed Assets—Net: To know much about this stuff I would need a list and details, also—if we are to loan money—an appraisal.

PAST BALANCE SHEETS

	YEAR 1	YEAR 2	YEAR 3	YEAR 4	YEAR 5
Cash	2,300	(2,000)	7,300	3,400	13,100
Accounts Receivable	18,000	32,000	47,000	61,000	78,000
Inventory—Finished Goods	10,000	20,000	30,000	40,000	50,000
—Raw Materials	15,000	23,000	28,000	38,000	46,000
—Work in Process	9,000	5,000	8,000	14,000	9,000
Claim—Income Taxes			1,800		
C/A	54,300	78,000	122,100	156,400	196,100
Fixed Assets—Net	24,300	27,200	34,600	112,300	119,600
Prepaid & Deferred Items	3,000	4,300	5,700	4,900	10,300
Other Assets	1,000	1,000	2,400	1,300	2,100
T/A	82,600	110,500	164,800	274,900	328,100
Notes Payable—Bank	14,000	12,900	45,100	58,000	88,000
Current Maturities	7,100	12,400	11,800	24,200	19,300
Accounts Payable	9,000	18,000	21,000	28,000	33,000
Accruals	4,400	6,100	11,300	8,900	12,400
Provision for Income Taxes	1,000	2,300		1,900	12,800
Due to Officers	3,100	3,100	13,100	15,800	16,700
C/L	38,600	54,800	102,300	136,800	182,200
Notes & Contracts—Deferred	14,000	13,000	20,000	38,000	27,000
Real Estate Mortgage—Deferred				51,000	46,000
D/I	14,000	13,000	20,000	89,000	73,000
T/L	52,600	67,800	122,300	225,800	255,200
Common Stock	10,000	10,000	10,000	10,000	10,000
Capital Surplus	10,000	10,000	10,000	10,000	10,000
Earned Surplus	10,000	22,700	22,500	29,100	52,900
NET WORTH	30,000	42,700	42,500	49,100	72,900
TOTAL LIAB. & NET WTH.	82,600	110,500	164,800	274,900	328,100

Exhibit 1

17

Prepaid and Deferred Items: This item has been growing regularly; I wonder if they had deferred some costs which should really have gone in as profit reduction items.

Notes Payable—Bank: Like so many of our growing young companies, this one seems to owe the bank steadily, and in increasingly larger amounts. . . . I must study their borrowing history to see if they are able to clean up at any time during the year. Also, I wonder how much money they need now, and what their repayment program is supposed to look like. . . .

Current Maturities: For some reason I see this item dropped in size this last year; I will want to compare this with the company's cash-flow-generation ability.

Accounts Payable: To interpret this item I will need to look at an aging of their accounts payable; the way many companies give credit these days it's a wonder anyone still needs to borrow money at the bank.

Accruals: Let's see; this item would consist of payroll taxes and things like that; we should make sure they are current on those items.

Provision for Income Taxes: It appears that they are making profits, and apparently more so all the time, since this is the largest provision they had to make over the past several years.

Due to Officers: Presumably we could get this subordinated to us.

Notes and Contracts—Deferred: We will need a schedule in order to properly interpret this item.

Real Estate Mortgage—Deferred: It is a good thing they are not looking for this mortgage right now; that type of money is currently particularly tight and they were certainly prudent in getting it a couple of years ago when it was easier to do so.

Common Stock: Presumably this is all owned by the company president and his wife, but I will want to verify this; also, I should probably find out if they have any arrangement whereby life insurance flows into the company in the event of the president's death, to buy out the estate, and also I might ask him about using our Trust Department in this connection.

Earned Surplus: This account is building up to a respectable size with additional profits. If he started with $20,000.00, as appears likely from looking at the common stock and capital surplus accounts, he has done rather well over the past few years. Of course, this could be a lot higher or lower depending on what kind of salary he has been taking out . . . I should find out about that.

Did any of the same thoughts that the banker had come to your mind? What came to your mind that the banker didn't think about? Do you see why this is a rather basic procedure which is followed in banks and similar organizations?

BALANCE SHEET PERCENTAGES

Exhibit 2 shows the distribution of assets as a percentage related to total assets, and the same thing for liabilities and net worth items. At times the banker will prepare

BALANCE SHEET PERCENTAGES

	YEAR 1	YEAR 2	YEAR 3	YEAR 4	YEAR 5
Cash	2.8	(1.8)	4.4	1.2	4.0
Accounts Receivable	21.9	28.9	28.5	22.3	23.8
Inventory—Finished Goods	12.2	18.2	18.2	14.6	15.2
—Raw Materials	18.2	20.9	17.0	13.9	14.0
—Work in Process	10.9	4.5	4.9	5.1	2.8
Claim—Income Taxes	—	—	1.1	—	—
C/A	66.0	70.7	74.1	57.1	59.8
Fixed Assets—Net	29.4	24.5	21.0	40.6	36.5
Prepaid & Deferred Items	3.5	3.9	3.5	1.8	3.1
Other Assets	1.1	.9	1.4	.5	.6
T/A	100.0	100.0	100.0	100.0	100.0
Notes Payable—Bank	16.9	11.7	27.4	21.1	26.8
Current Maturities	8.6	11.2	7.2	8.8	5.9
Accounts Payable	10.9	16.3	12.7	10.2	10.1
Accurals	5.3	5.5	6.9	3.3	3.8
Provision for Income Taxes	1.2	2.1	—	.7	3.9
Due to Officers	3.9	2.8	7.9	5.8	5.1
C/L	46.8	49.6	62.1	49.9	55.6
Notes & Contracts—Deferred	16.9	11.8	12.1	13.8	8.2
Real Estate Mortgage—Deferred	—	—	—	18.5	14.0
D/L	16.9	11.8	12.1	32.3	22.2
T/L	63.7	61.4	74.2	82.2	77.8
Common Stock	12.1	9.0	6.1	3.6	3.0
Capital Surplus	12.1	9.0	6.1	3.6	3.0
Earned Surplus	12.1	20.6	13.6	10.6	16.2
NET WORTH	36.3	38.6	25.8	17.8	22.2
TOTAL LIAB. & NET WTH.	100.0	100.0	100.0	100.0	100.0

Exhibit 2

exhibits similar to this and use them to compare one particular company's figures with those for the industry, as made available to the bank through various agencies. In other words, this answers such questions as, "Does this company have more or less current assets than is typical for its type? What about fixed assets; is its debt load in keeping with the industry or is it in worse shape?"

Many industries prepare figures of this type and distribute them to their members; it is certainly useful to compare your company with industry averages if these are available.

Scanning this exhibit, one might notice first that current assets, which now represent about 60 percent of assets, used to represent somewhat more than that. Also, current liabilities, which used to run about 47 percent, are now up to 56 percent. It might also come to one's notice that net worth used to represent 36 percent of total liabilities and net worth, whereas it now represents only 22 percent; in other words, total liabilities have been growing at a more rapid rate than have net worth accounts; that doesn't sound too healthy, does it?

BALANCE SHEET TRENDS

This type of document (Exhibit 3) is, normally, not prepared by a bank. Nevertheless, it is a very useful type of analysis because it shows "year one" as being 100 percent, and points out how various items in the balance sheet have changed since that year.

BALANCE SHEET TRENDS

	YEAR 1	YEAR 2	YEAR 3	YEAR 4	YEAR 5
Cash	100.0	87	317	148	570
Accounts Receivable	100.0	178	261	339	433
Inventory—Finished Goods	100.0	200	300	400	500
—Raw Materials	100.0	153	187	253	307
—Work in Process	100.0	56	89	156	100
Claim—Income Taxes	—	—	—	—	—
C/A	100.0	144	225	287	360
Fixed Assets—Net	100.0	112	143	461	491
Prepaid & Deferred Items	100.0	144	190	164	344
Other Assets	100.0	100	240	130	210
T/A	100.0	134	199	333	399
Notes Payable—Bank	100.0	92	323	415	631
Current Maturities	100.0	174	167	341	273
Accounts Payable	100.0	200	234	311	367
Accurals	100.0	139	257	202	282
Provision for Income Taxes	100.0	230	—	190	1,280
Due to Officers	100.0	100	424	511	539
C/L	100.0	142	266	355	474
Notes & Contracts—Deferred	100.0	93	143	272	193
Real Estate Mortgage—Deferred	—	—	—	—	—
D/L	100.0	93	143	635	522
T/L	100.0	139	233	432	488
Common Stock	100.0	100	100	100	100
Capital Surplus	100.0	100	100	100	100
Earned Surplus	100.0	227	225	291	529
NET WORTH	100.0	142	141	164	243
TOTAL LIAB. & NET WTH.	100.0	134	199	333	399

Exhibit 3

For example, note that total assets increased from 100 percent to almost 400 percent. Next, it is reasonable to look up and down the line and see what is growing as fast as total assets and what is growing slower than total assets.

In this connection, note that the items which have been growing faster than the total position of the company are as follows: cash, receivables, finished goods inventory, fixed assets, notes payable—bank, income taxes, and due to officers. And, of course there is a real estate mortgage where there was once none.

Similarly, we note that the following items grew less rapidly than did total company position: raw material inventories, work in process inventories, prepaid and deferred items, other assets, current maturities, accounts payable, accruals and, finally, net worth.

By the nature of things, it would not be natural to expect every item in the business balance sheet to move ahead at the same rate. But it does serve some purpose to note that the finished goods inventory is rising relatively faster than the other elements of inventory; that the company might be keeping too much money in cash; that fixed assets have grown somewhat faster than the business as a whole; that there is relatively great reliance on the notes payable bank; and that profits, as reflected in net worth, are not keeping pace with the total growth of the company. This last statement is made despite the fact that earned surplus, the part of the balance sheet that reflects profit, is 529 percent of what it was at the beginning year and totals are only 400 percent; nevertheless, note that net worth *as a whole* has not kept pace.

Exhibits such as this are relatively simple to prepare, and very valuable in that with each year's addition one provides new insights.

CURRENT RATIO

The current ratio is perhaps the most popular ratio used by people who analyze financial statements. It is prepared by dividing the current assets of the company by its current liabilities for a particular date (see Exhibit 4).

CURRENT RATIOS

YEAR	CURRENT ASSETS @ Y/E	CURRENT LIAB. @ Y/E	C/A DIV. BY C/L
1	$ 54,300	$ 38,600	1.41
2	78,000	54,800	1.42
3	122,100	102,300	1.20
4	156,400	136,800	1.14
5	196,100	182,100	1.08

Exhibit 4

In looking at the current ratio of the company we are studying a period of five years, and we note that it is less liquid than five years ago. This trend will not be interpreted favorably by the banker or whoever is looking at it. One would prefer to see an increasingly liquid situation.

DEBT TO WORTH RATIO

Probably the second most popular ratio used by bankers and others is the debt to worth ratio, which is determined by dividing the total liabilities of the company by the net worth of the company (see Exhibit 5).

	DEBT TO WORTH RATIOS		
YEAR	TOTAL DEBT @ Y/E	NET WORTH @ Y/E	DEBT DIV. BY WORTH
1	$ 52,600	$ 30,000	1.75
2	67,800	42,700	1.58
3	122,300	42,500	2.85
4	225,800	49,100	2.18
5	255,200	72,900	3.50

Exhibit 5

In looking at the Exhibit, it will be noted that the company's debt to worth ratio has been increasing from year to year. In other words, at "year five" there were three and one-half times the net worth in total liabilities as compared to exactly half that ratio in "year one." Generally speaking, the heavier the reliance on debt, the worse it is as far as the commercial banker is concerned.

DAYS' SALES IN ACCOUNTS RECEIVABLE

Over the years there has developed a particular computation which is used to determine the quality of the accounts receivable as reflected on the balance sheet. This computation involves comparing the amount of accounts receivable on a particular balance sheet with the amount of sales that have taken place during a particular period. On annual statements, this figure is determined by dividing the accounts receivable figure shown on the year-end statement by the sales figure as shown on the profit and loss statement. As you will note from Exhibit 6, when $18,000.00 was divided by $100,000.00 for year one, .18 resulted. ".18" was then multiplied by 360 days and the answer "65" resulted. The Exhibit shows that the company's investment in accounts receivable has really been on a rather steady basis, and if one were to be doing some projecting, it would appear that 57 days' accounts receivable would be a reasonable basis on which to plan. (Incidentally, if you wanted to determine the days' sales in accounts receivable in connection with a *monthly* financial statement, the same procedure would be followed, up to a point. That is, accounts receivable on the balance sheet would be divided by the sales figure for the *month;* the resulting figure then being multiplied by *thirty* days.)

This is a very useful index and should be computed by management at all times. It gives management a basis for measuring the effectiveness of its credit department function, among other things.

DAYS' SALES IN ACCOUNTS RECEIVABLE

YEAR	SALES	Y/E ACCOUNTS RECEIVABLE	REC. DIV. BY SALES	PREV. COL. × 360 DAYS
1	$100,000	$18,000	.18	65 days
2	200,000	32,000	.16	57
3	300,000	47,000	.16	57
4	400,000	61,000	.15	54
5	500,000	78,000	.16	57

Exhibit 6

DAYS' COST OF GOODS SOLD IN INVENTORY

A computation similar to that just discussed above for accounts receivable and sales is used to determine the relative amount of inventory efficiency. In this instance, the inventory is divided by the *cost* of sales, and the resulting figure multiplied by 360 days to determine the number of days of costs that are in inventory.

We note in this case, from looking at Exhibit 7, that the company has improved its efficiency over the years. It used to carry 155 days of inventory and now only carries 97 days. This reflects a healthy trend. (If one wishes to determine this same figure on the basis of a *monthly* statement, the inventory shown on the balance sheet is divided by the cost of sales for the *month,* and the resulting figure is then multiplied by *thirty* days.)

DAYS' COST OF GOODS SOLD IN INVENTORY

YEAR	COST OF SALES	Y/E INVENTORY	Y/E INV. DIV. BY COST OF SALES	PREV. COL. × 360 DAYS
1	$ 80.000	$ 34,000	.43	155
2	165,500	48,000	.29	104
3	237,500	66,000	.28	101
4	331,000	92,000	.28	101
5	385,900	105,000	.27	97

Exhibit 7

This computation is very useful in keeping an eye on inventory levels, among other things.

ANALYSIS OF CHANGES IN WORKING CAPITAL

Working capital, a calculation that is always made at the bank or by others working with your financial statements, is determined by subtracting current liabilities

ANALYSIS OF CHANGES IN WORKING CAPITAL

	YEAR 1	YEAR 2	YEAR 3	YEAR 4	YEAR 5
Current Assets	$54,300	$78,000	$122,100	$156,400	$196,100
Current Liabilities	38,600	54,800	102,300	136,800	182,200
Working Capital	15,700	23,200	19,800	19,600	13,900
		15,700	23,200	19,800	19,600
Net Increase or (Decrease) in W/C	Not Avail.	7,500	(3,400)	(200)	(5,700)
INCREASES in Working Capital:					
Earnings		12,700		6,600	23,800
Decrease in Other Assets				1,100	
Decrease in Prepd. & Def.				800	
Increase in Notes & Cont. Def.			7,000	18,000	
New Real Estate Mtge., Def.				51,000	
TOTAL		12,700	7,000	77,500	23,800
DECREASES in Working Capital:					
Loss			200		
Fixed Asset Additions, Net					
of Depreciation		2,900	7,400	77,700	7,300
Increase, Prepd. & Def.		1,300	1,400		5,400
Increase in Other Assets			1,400		800
Reduction, Notes & Cont. Def.		1,000			11,000
Reduction, R. E. Mtge.					5,000
TOTAL		5,200	10,400	77,700	29,500
NET INCREASE OR (DECREASE)		7,500	(3,400)	(200)	(5,700)

Exhibit 8

24

from current assets. This figure represents the excess of the latter over the former. The higher the figure, the more liquid is your company, the stronger your current position, and the better things are where the bank is concerned.

Exhibit 8 shows the calculation of working capital for five years for the company we are studying. Note it also analyzes the increases and decreases in working capital for each year, showing what factors tended to cause the increase or decrease in that item.

This analysis is prepared by looking at a balance sheet *spread,* such as that drawn up earlier and reviewed. It is especially interesting to note what increases working capital and what decreases it. In "year four," for example, it is clear that the company increased working capital by going out and getting some additional debt ($18,000.00 and $51,000.00). In the current year, "year five," however, note that earnings is the only factor that worked to increase working capital.

The section entitled "Decreases in Working Capital" explains what has been going on in terms of investment of funds that decrease working capital. Note especially that the addition of fixed assets has regularly pulled it down. Note also that beginning in "year five" the reduction of the liabilities taken on in "year four" begins to affect working capital.

This type of analysis has become so popular that many times certified public accountants now include a statement of this type with their audit report. This is the Exhibit that serves to answer the question, "Things have been going along well in terms of profits, but where is the money (cash) going?"

EARNINGS ON TOTAL ASSETS EMPLOYED

This is a ratio which is sometimes calculated and shows the relationship of earnings after income taxes to total assets employed in the business. Note that in Exhibit 9

EARNINGS ON TOTAL ASSETS EMPLOYED

YEAR	NET EARNINGS	TOTAL ASSETS @ Y/E	NET ENGS. DIV. BY TOTAL ASSETS
1	$ 6,000	$ 82,600	7.3%
2	12,700	110,500	11.5
3	(200)	164,800	—
4	6,600	274,900	2.4
5	23,800	328,100	7.3

Exhibit 9

total assets at year end were used; actually, it would be more accurate to use the beginning total asset figure added to the total assets at the end of the year and divided by two—or the average total assets. The higher this figure is the better.

EARNINGS ON NET WORTH

Exhibit 10 uses the procedures suggested above and relates an *average* net worth to net earnings for the period. This is a critical calculation, in that it shows what is earned on the net worth; unsatisfactory results as to this calculation are a real sign of sickness. In this case, the company is undercapitalized; that is, the company is showing a high percentage of return on net worth because the net worth is so small in relationship to the total assets. These are merely two sides of the same coin.

EARNINGS ON NET WORTH

YEAR	NET EARNINGS	NET WORTH @ BEG. OF YR.	NET WORTH @ END OF YR.	AVG. N. W.	ENGS. ON WORTH
1	$ 6,000	$24,000	$30,000	$27,000	22.2%
2	12,700	30,000	42,700	36,300	35.0
3	(200)	42,700	42,500	42,600	—
4	6,600	42,500	49,100	45,800	14.4
5	23,800	49,100	72,900	61,000	38.9

Exhibit 10

This completes the balance sheet exhibits and next we will examine, one by one, the profit and loss statement exhibits.

PROFIT AND LOSS SPREAD

This alignment of figures side by side resembles that of the balance sheet spread, except of course the format is different because we are dealing with the profit and loss statement and not a balance sheet (see Exhibit 11).

First, we note that sales have been increasing steadily. Also, we note that costs and expenses have been increasing regularly. Aside from this, it is difficult to make too much of this exhibit because it does not show percentage relationships. That is why banks always utilize percentages, as we will note in the next Exhibit.

PROFIT AND LOSS STATEMENTS—PERCENTAGE COMPARISON

You will notice in Exhibit 12 that *gross* sales equaled 100 percent. Sometimes accountants and bankers use a different system, whereby *net* sales equal 100 percent. The difference is negligible and it really is a theoretical argument as to which is the more popular. The author happens to prefer to call gross sales 100 percent and has accordingly used this system.

In any event, first we will note that returns and allowances have averaged some-

PAST PROFIT AND LOSS STATEMENTS

	YEAR 1	YEAR 2	YEAR 3	YEAR 4	YEAR 5
GROSS SALES	$100,000	$200,000	$300,000	$400,000	$500,000
(Less: Returns & Allowances)	(1,000)	(1,500)	(3,500)	(3,000)	(6,100)
NET SALES	$ 99,000	$198,500	$296,500	$397,000	$493,900
COST OF GOODS SOLD:					
Cost of Goods Manufactured:					
Change, WIP Inventory	$ 2,000	$ (4,000)	$ 3,000	$ 6,000	$ (5,000)
Materials	40,000	80,000	121,000	160,000	183,000
Labor	30,000	61,000	90,000	141,000	156,000
Manufacturing Expenses	8,000	28,500	23,500	24,000	51,900
TOTAL	$ 80,000	$165,500	$237,500	$331,000	$385,900
Beg. Inventory, Finished Goods	$ 10,000	$ 10,000	$ 20,000	$ 30,000	$ 40,000
Cost of Goods Manufactured	80,000	165,500	237,500	331,000	385,900
SUBTOTAL	$ 90,000	$175,500	$257,500	$361,000	$425,900
(Less: End. Inv. Fin. Goods)	(10,000)	(20,000)	(30,000)	(40,000)	(50,000)
TOTAL	$ 80,000	$155,500	$227,500	$321,000	$375,900
GROSS PROFIT	$ 19,000	$ 43,000	$ 69,000	$ 76,000	$118,000
EXPENSES:					
Sales Expense	$ 7,000	$ 13,000	$ 22,000	$ 26,000	$ 31,000
General & Admin. Expense	8,000	16,000	37,000	40,000	47,000
TOTAL	$ 15,000	$ 29,000	$ 59,000	$ 66,000	$ 78,000
OPERATING PROFIT	$ 4,000	$ 14,000	$ 10,000	$ 10,000	$ 40,000
OTHER INCOME (OTHER CHARGES)—NET	3,000	1,000	(12,000)	(1,500)	(3,400)
PROFIT BEFORE INCOME TAXES	$ 7,000	$ 15,000	$ (2,000)	$ 8,500	$ 36,600
PROVISION FOR INCOME TAXES	1,000	2,300	(1,800)	1,900	12,800
PROFIT AFTER INCOME TAXES	$ 6,000	$ 12,700	$ (200)	$ 6,600	$ 23,800

Exhibit 11

PERCENTAGE COMPARISON—PROFIT AND LOSS STATEMENTS

	YEAR 1	YEAR 2	YEAR 3	YEAR 4	YEAR 5
GROSS SALES	100.0	100.0	100.0	100.0	100.0
(Returns & Allowances)	(1.0)	(.8)	(1.1)	(.7)	(1.2)
NET SALES	99.0	99.2	98.9	99.3	98.8
COST OF GOODS SOLD:					
Cost of Goods Mfd.:					
Change, WIP Inven.	2.0	(2.0)	1.0	1.5	(1.0)
Materials	40.0	40.0	40.5	40.0	36.5
Labor	30.0	30.5	30.0	35.3	31.3
Mfg. Expenses	8.0	14.2	7.9	6.0	10.3
TOTAL	80.0	82.7	79.4	82.8	77.1
Cost of Goods Sold	80.0	77.7	75.9	80.3	75.2
GROSS PROFIT	19.0	21.5	23.0	19.0	23.6
EXPENSES:					
Sales Expense	7.0	6.5	7.4	6.5	6.2
G. & A. Expense	8.0	8.0	12.3	10.0	9.4
TOTAL	15.0	14.5	19.7	16.5	15.6
OPERATING PROFIT	4.0	7.0	3.3	2.5	8.0
OTHER INCOME—(OTHER CHARGES)—NET	3.0	.5	(4.0)	(.4)	(.7)
PROFIT BEFORE INCOME TAXES	7.0	7.5	(.7)	2.1	7.3

Exhibit 12

thing like 1 percent of sales. Sometimes an unsatisfactory turn in operations shows up in this item. It is always subject to critical review by lenders, because they want to know how much of what is originally in accounts receivable turns into something else. The next percentage that everyone looks at is the gross profit percentage. This percentage will not only be compared with that for other customers which the bank has, but with industry figures. Other percentages are helpful in looking at trends, but only the sales expense is a variable that should show a definite relationship with sales; hopefully, "G. & A." expense would show a declining percentage relationship to sales as sales increase.

Finally, it is the profit figure on sales that people are interested in. In this particular case, we have stopped at profit *before* income taxes; in some cases, people go ahead and figure income taxes as a percentage and then show a profit *after* those taxes. In the author's opinion the figure is less meaningful than profit before income taxes, for analytical purposes, and accordingly it has not been included here.

TREND STUDY—PROFIT AND LOSS STATEMENTS

Exhibit 13 is similar to a balance sheet trend Exhibit that we have already discussed, in that it starts out with year one being 100 percent and shows the trend in the various items from that year to the present year. Again, the general way to look at this is to see what sales have done, and then compare other items in relationship.

TREND STUDY—PROFIT AND LOSS STATEMENTS

(YEAR 1 = 100)

	YEAR 1	YEAR 2	YEAR 3	YEAR 4	YEAR 5
Gross Sales	100	200	300	400	500
Returns & Allowances	100	150	350	300	610
Materials	100	200	303	400	457
Labor	100	214	300	470	520
Manufacturing Expenses	100	356	295	300	648
Cost of Goods Manufactured	100	217	298	415	485
Cost of Goods Sold	100	194	295	403	472
Gross Profit	100	226	364	400	621
Sales Expense	100	186	314	373	444
G. & A. Expense	100	200	463	500	589
Total Expenses	100	194	394	441	521
Operating Profit	100	350	250	250	1,000
O/I–O/C	100	33	(400)	(50)	(114)
Profit Before I/T	100	214	(29)	122	522

Exhibit 13

Sales, for example, are 500 percent and profits before income taxes slightly better, or 522 percent. Sales expense has run somewhat less than the trend, G. & A. expense somewhat higher. The gross profit has grown in excess of the 500 percent trend. Also, returns and allowances have run in excess of the trend.

This type of analysis is very helpful in spotting trends and should be prepared by the company periodically.

ANALYSIS—SALES BY MONTHS

Even businesses which one does not think of as being seasonal do have trends from one year to the next as to how much business occurs during a particular month of a year. These facts are particularly important in connection with borrowing money. Exhibit 14, on the accompanying page, has broken down sales month by month for five years, and shows the percentage of total sales for the year that occurred in a particular month. This approach makes it easy to spot trends, such as when business drops at a particular time of the year rather regularly.

PERCENTAGE CHANGE—GROSS SALES

When discussing sales, one of the most common references is to the amount of increase, in terms of percentages, over the prior year. This information is gathered

ANALYSIS—SALES BY MONTHS

YEAR		JAN.	FEB.	MAR.	APRIL	MAY	JUNE	JULY	AUG.	SEPT.	OCT.	NOV.	DEC.	TOTALS
1		$5,000	10,000	7,000	7,000	9,000	5,000	10,000	12,000	8,000	6,000	10,000	11,000	100,000
	%	5	10	7	7	9	5	10	12	8	6	10	11	100
2		$9,000	13,000	10,000	11,000	14,000	18,000	13,000	19,000	21,000	27,000	32,000	13,000	200,000
	%	4½	6½	5	5½	7	9	6½	9½	10½	13½	16	6½	100
3		$24,000	29,000	35,000	27,000	25,000	30,000	20,000	15,000	28,000	11,000	27,000	29,000	300,000
	%	8½	9½	11½	9	8½	10	6½	5	9½	3½	9	9½	100
4		$31,000	31,000	36,000	22,000	29,000	21,000	38,000	41,000	43,000	36,000	30,000	42,000	400,000
	%	7½	7½	9	5½	7½	5½	9½	10	11	9	7½	10½	100
5		$38,000	39,000	42,000	26,000	35,000	33,000	41,000	53,000	48,000	48,000	47,000	50,000	500,000
	%	7½	8	8½	5	7	6½	8	11	9½	9½	9½	10	100

Exhibit 14

together in Exhibit 15. Percentages have a way of playing tricks: a company can express as a matter of intent that it intends to grow 20 percent each year; actually this would become a little hard to do as total dollar figures grow.

PERCENTAGE CHANGE—GROSS SALES

YEAR	$ GROSS SALES	$ CHANGE	% CHANGE OVER PRIOR YEAR
1	100,000	27,000[a]	+ 37
2	200,000	100,000	+100
3	300,000	100,000	+ 50
4	400,000	100,000	+ 33
5	500,000	100,000	+ 25

[a]Past records indicate sales for *first* year of business, before "Year 1," were $73,000.

Exhibit 15

ANALYSIS—SALES BY SALESMEN

Exhibit 16 breaks down the sales as to *salesmen*. This type of information is particularly important for management. Note that it involves digging a little deeper and going down another layer to develop information. This is typical of the figure approach to business: first you start out with the broad picture, and then you keep digging down below this figure to get more details. Increasingly, the story—whatever that is—unfolds.

ANALYSIS—SALES BY SALESMEN

	YEAR 1	YEAR 2	YEAR 3	YEAR 4	YEAR 5
Salesman Smith	100,000	60,000	40,000	130,000	150,000
Salesman Jones	——	100,000	205,000	180,000	250,000
"House Accounts"	——	40,000	30,000	40,000	42,000
Agents	——	——	20,000	35,000	50,000
Misc.[a]	——	——	5,000	15,000	8,000
TOTALS	100,000	200,000	300,000	400,000	500,000

[a]Incomplete records made a "plug" nesessary.

Exhibit 16

In this particular case, it is interesting to note that the rather steady progress of the company has resulted from some rather irregular results from salesmen. For example, look at salesman Smith. At the end of "year three," he might have been a candidate for dismissal; and his sales have dropped steadily from years one to three. Note, however, that he recovered and produced well in years four and five. Note also, however, that salesman Jones has come up to be the leading salesman and that he was hired after salesman Smith. It is also interesting to note that house accounts contributed a rather steady amount to the business, agents for an increasing amount of it, and miscellaneous accounts for some sales. That "miscellaneous" category always invites examination, and one is prompted to ask what kind of sales fall in that category. . . .

AVERAGE—RETURNS AND ALLOWANCES

Exhibit 17 focuses attention again on returns and allowances on a percentage basis relative to sales. It computes an average, which might be helpful in terms of projecting.

AVERAGE—RETURNS AND ALLOWANCES		GROSS PROFIT—PERCENT TO SALES	
YEAR	% TO SALES	YEAR	%
1	1.0	1	19.0
2	.8	2	21.5
3	1.1	3	23.0
4	.7	4	19.0
5	1.2	5	23.6
DIV. BY 5 = AVG.	4.8	TOTAL	106.1
TOTAL	1.0	DIV. BY 5 = AVG.	21.2

Exhibit 17	Exhibit 18

GROSS PROFIT—PERCENT TO SALES

Exhibit 18 shows gross profit as a percent to sales. It also computes an average. This is a critical element in projecting future operations, and it is to be looked at from several standpoints. It is very dangerous simply to accept an average gross profit figure to use in projecting financial statements.

AVERAGE—MATERIAL COSTS

Note that in Exhibit 19 material costs are related not only to sales but also to *total* costs. In other words, it is one thing to say that on the average material costs run 39.4 percent of sales, and it is quite another thing to say that 49 percent are material costs. Both of these relationships need to be studied in connection with the projection of financial statements and also with an appraisal of what has gone on in the past.

AVERAGE—MATERIAL COSTS		
YEAR	% TO SALES	% TO TOTAL COSTS
1	40.0	50.0
2	40.0	48.1
3	40.5	51.0
4	40.0	48.3
5	36.5	47.6
TOTAL	197.0	245.0
DIV. BY 5 = AVG.	39.4	49.0

Exhibit 19

AVERAGE—LABOR COSTS		
YEAR	% TO SALES	% TO TOTAL COSTS
1	30.0	37.5
2	30.5	36.7
3	30.0	38.0
4	35.3	42.6
5	31.3	40.5
TOTAL	157.1	195.3
DIV. BY 5 = AVG.	31.4	39.1

Exhibit 20

AVERAGE—LABOR COSTS

For the same reasons that we are interested in looking at material costs both in relationship to sales and to total cost, we are interested in looking at labor costs relative to sales and to total costs. Both of these are computed and averaged in Exhibit 20.

ANALYSIS—LABOR AND MATERIAL RELATIONSHIPS

Exhibit 21 shows the relationship between labor and material costs. Management should be aware of trends and relationships such as this. Sometimes a particular policy designed to lower this relationship will be adopted and will result in purchasing more outside materials.

ANALYSIS—LABOR AND MATERIAL RELATIONSHIPS					
	YEAR 1	YEAR 2	YEAR 3	YEAR 4	YEAR 5
Materials	$40,000	$80,000	$121,000	$160,000	$183,000
Labor	30,000	61,000	90,000	141,000	156,000
Labor, as a % of Materials	75%	76%	75%	88%	85%

Exhibit 21

AVERAGE—MANUFACTURING EXPENSES

Exhibit 22 shows the manufacturing expenses for the past five years, together with the average. Also, the relationship of these expenses both to sales and total costs is shown. Often management utilizes this information in connection with the allocation of overhead.

AVERAGE—MANUFACTURING EXPENSES

YEAR	$	% TO SALES	% TO TOTAL COSTS
1	8,000	8.0	10.0
2	28,500	14.2	17.2
3	23,500	7.9	9.9
4	24,000	6.0	7.3
5	51,900	10.3	13.3
TOTAL	135,900	46.4	57.7
DIV. BY 5 = AVG.	27,180	9.3	11.5

Exhibit 22

MANUFACTURING EXPENSES DETAILED

Exhibit 23 shows the detail of what made up manufacturing expenses for each of the past five years. This basic type of exhibit is very useful and it is referred to regularly as a whole in analysis of the profit and loss statement.

PAST MANUFACTURING EXPENSES—DETAILED
(DOLLARS)

	YEAR 1	YEAR 2	YEAR 3	YEAR 4	YEAR 5
Supervis. Salaries	4,500	6,500	7,500	7,500	16,000
Indirect Labor	——	10,100	7,200	4,100	13,500
Depreciation	2,900	3,100	4,200	7,900	8,300
Repairs & Mtce.	——	300	800	300	1,400
Supplies	200	1,700	2,100	3,000	5,600
Payroll Taxes	300	1,100	800	600	1,300
Engineering Exp.	——	5,300	600	400	5,200
Misc.	100	400	300	200	600
TOTAL	8,000	28,500	23,500	24,000	51,900

Exhibit 23

Marked increases are apparent for supervisory salaries, indirect labor, repairs and maintenance, supplies and engineering expenses. Supervisory salaries more than doubled from "year four" to "year five." Indirect labor for "year five" is more than three times what this same item ran for "year four." Engineering expense runs more than twelve times the "year four" expenditure in "year five."

Clearly, much of what is changing in the company's cost picture has to do with manufacturing expenses, and the trends expressed in this particular exhibit, if projected into the future, are not too good. . . .

ANALYSIS—LABOR AND MANUFACTURING EXPENSE RELATIONSHIP

Labor as well as manufacturing expenses for the past five years is shown in Exhibit 24. Also shown is the percentage relationship between manufacturing expenses and labor. This basic relationship is often used by management in allocation of overhead.

ANALYSIS—LABOR AND MANUFACTURING EXPENSE RELATIONSHIPS

	YEAR 1	YEAR 2	YEAR 3	YEAR 4	YEAR 5
Labor	$30,000	$61,000	$90,000	$141,000	$156,000
Mfg. Exp.	8,000	28,500	23,500	24,000	51,900
Mfg. Exp., as % of Labor	27%	47%	26%	17%	33%

Exhibit 24

SALES EXPENSES

Exhibit 25 shows what the sales expenses have run for each of the last five years, the percentage relationship to sales, and the average for the period. In preparing budgets and projections this type of relationship is most meaningful because sales expenses should relate directly to sales results.

AVERAGE—SALES EXPENSE

YEAR	$	% TO SALES
1	7,000	7.0
2	13,000	6.5
3	22,000	7.4
4	26,000	6.5
5	31,000	6.2
TOTAL	99,000	33.6
DIV. BY 5 = AVG.	19,800	6.7

Exhibit 25

SALES EXPENSES DETAILED

The details that comprise sales expenses are shown in Exhibit 26. Percentage relationships are again reflected, because the connection between sales expenses and sales results is particularly direct.

PAST SALES EXPENSES—DETAILED

(SHOWING $ AND % TO SALES)	YEAR 1	YEAR 2	YEAR 3	YEAR 4	YEAR 5
Salaries and Commissions	5,500	10,300	14,600	16,700	19,400
	5.5%	5.2%	4.9%	4.2%	3.9%
Travel & Entertainment	900	1,800	2,400	3,200	4,100
	.9%	.9%	.8%	.8%	.8%
Advertising	100	100	3,500	4,400	5,300
Delivery Expense	300	500	1,100	1,300	1,700
Depreciation	200	300	400	400	500
TOTAL	7,000	13,000	22,000	26,000	31,000
	7.0%	6.5%	7.4%	6.5%	6.2%

Exhibit 26

GENERAL AND ADMINISTRATIVE EXPENSES

Exhibit 27 shows what the total of general and administrative expenses have been for each of the past five years, together with the relationship of such expenses to sales and also the average for the five-year period. Often the objective is to have general and administrative expenses, in a situation where sales are rising, represent an increasingly *smaller* percentage of sales.

AVERAGE—GENERAL AND ADMINISTRATIVE EXPENSES

YEAR	$	% TO SALES
1	8,000	8.0
2	16,000	8.0
3	37,000	12.3
4	40,000	10.0
5	47,000	9.4
TOTAL	148,000	47.7
DIV. BY 5 = AVG.	29,600	9.5

Exhibit 27

GENERAL AND ADMINISTRATIVE EXPENSES DETAILED

Exhibit 28 shows the many items that went together to make up general and administrative expenses in each of the past five years. Again, this type of Exhibit is a basic proposition and is often referred to in connection with the preparation of projections. A study of this Exhibit tells us that these expenses are controlled, and that in terms of absolute dollars, executive salaries and office salaries are rising. Also, it tells us that our interest expense is rising at a very rapid pace, reflecting the additional debt that has been taken on.

PAST GENERAL AND ADMINISTRATIVE EXPENSES—DETAILED

	YEAR 1	YEAR 2	YEAR 3	YEAR 4	YEAR 5
Executive Salaries	4,500	6,000	12,300	13,000	14,500
Office Salaries	1,300	3,000	8,600	7,300	9,400
Office Supplies & Stationery	100	300	400	600	700
Postage	100	200	200	200	400
Telephone	300	500	900	1,100	1,200
Professional Services	300	600	1,200	1,400	1,200
Insurance—General	100	400	1,100	1,800	1,800
Insurance—Employee Hospitalization	—	—	700	800	900
Payroll Taxes	200	400	700	900	1,100
Personal Property Taxes	100	300	400	400	400
Real Estate Taxes	—	—	—	900	1,200
Bad Debts	—	1,100	3,100	1,100	600
Collection Expense	—	100	600	200	100
Dues & Subscriptions	100	200	300	200	200
Bank Charges	100	200	300	300	300
Depreciation	100	100	100	200	200
Interest	400	1,800	4,800	8,300	12,000
Utilities	300	500	700	800	700
Repairs & Maintenance	—	200	400	300	100
Misc.	—	100	200	200	—
	8,000	16,000	37,000	40,000	47,000

Exhibit 28

OTHER INCOME (OTHER CHARGES)

Exhibit 29 reflects the miscellaneous type of income and charges that have occurred during the past five years. Reference is often made to an exhibit like this when analyzing a consolidated report, to see what the particularly unusual items were.

CASH FLOW

"Cash flow" is the combination of profits and depreciation, and any other non-cash items. It is important because it gives us an idea of the debt repayment ability of a company. Exhibit 30 shows what has gone to make up the cash flow for this company for the past five years.

PAST OTHER INCOME (OTHER CHARGES)

	YEAR 1	YEAR 2	YEAR 3	YEAR 4	YEAR 5
Gain, Sales of Assets	2,900	600	100	—	—
Loss, Sale of Assets	—	—	(300)	(1,500)	(1,700)
Fire Loss, Net	—	—	(11,000)	—	—
Misc. Income	100	500	—	—	—
Misc. Charges	—	(100)	(800)	—	(1,700)
	3,000	1,000	(12,000)	(1,500)	(3,400)

Exhibit 29

CASH FLOW—PAST PERIODS

	YEAR 1	YEAR 2	YEAR 3	YEAR 4	YEAR 5
PROFIT	6,000	12,700	(200)	6,600	23,800
DEPRECIATION:					
Mfg. Expenses	2,900	3,100	4,200	7,900	8,300
Sales Expenses	200	300	400	400	500
G. & A. Expenses	100	100	100	200	200
CASH FLOW	9,200	16,200	4,500	15,100	32,800

Exhibit 30

6
Where Are We?

To develop creativeness, the mind needs not only to be exercised, but to be filled with material out of which ideas can best be formed.

—Page 70, *Applied Imagination,*
by ALEX F. OSBORN,
Charles Scribner's Sons, 1957.

IN THE LAST CHAPTER WE TOOK A PRETTY INTENSIVE LOOK AT "WHERE we've been"; now it is time to take an equally hard look at just where we *are*. Now, having accumulated a lot of historical data (like the doctor who has finished taking your history), we are ready to move on and complete the other steps necessary for a good "current physical." Actually, the medical analogy breaks down somewhat, because in the process of looking back (as in the last chapter), we also looked at the most recent past and made various tests on the latest data available, so it would be more accurate to say that we have completed the history portion of the physical *and* a series of tests. (With figures, it is easy to go back and apply the tests—which of course you couldn't do for a physical examination.)

In any event, the financial statement that tells us "where we are" is the latest, most current *balance sheet;* in the present instance this happens also to be the last one considered under "history." Exhibit 31 is this balance sheet, and we shall use it as a point of departure in the discussion in this chapter of "where we are."

The basic objective of this rather thorough review of our current position is to bring freshly to mind all of the many facets of the operation—prompted by reference

CURRENT BALANCE SHEET

Cash	$ 13,100
Accounts Receivable	78,000
Inventory—Finished Goods	50,000
—Raw Materials	46,000
—Work in Process	9,000
CURRENT ASSETS	$196,100
Fixed Assets—Net	119,600
Prepaid and Deferred Items	10,300
Other Assets	2,100
TOTAL ASSETS	$328,100
Note Payable—Bank	$ 88,000
Current Maturities	19,300
Accounts Payable	33,000
Accruals	12,400
Provision for Income Taxes	12,800
Due to Officers	16,700
CURRENT LIABILITIES	$182,200
Notes & Contracts—Deferred	27,000
Real Estate Mortgage—Deferred	46,000
DEFFERED LIABILITIES	$ 73,000
TOTAL LIABILITIES	$255,200
Common Stock	$ 10,000
Capital Surplus	10,000
Earned Surplus	52,900
NET WORTH	$ 72,900
TOTAL LIABILITIES & NET WORTH	$328,100

Exhibit 31

to the balance sheet—so that all facts and figures appropriate to the subject are readily at hand and on tap, as a sound basis for a projection or forecast of the future.

In the last chapter we "wore the banker's hat" for awhile, and looked over part of our financial history much as the banker might do it. Having completed a "panoramic" shot of our past, we now focus close up on the present—the latest financial statement. This closeup view will bring to mind many thoughts and ideas stemming from a careful consideration of each balance sheet account. Using the balance sheet as a checklist, we will seek to bring to mind anything and everything that might be pertinent to the asset or liability under consideration, from the viewpoint of a banker or other lender, and from the standpoint of someone who wants to be ready to answer questions from such a lender.

CASH

Where are we banking, and why? Is the service satisfactory? Are we following prudent procedures as to who can sign checks? Who reconciles the bank statement? Have our auditors ever made recommendations about our internal procedures for cash

AGING OF ACCOUNTS RECEIVABLE

CUSTOMER, ADDRESS	TOTAL OWING	0–30 DAYS	30–60 DAYS	60–90 DAYS	90–120 DAYS	OLDER . . . .
Acme Distributing Co. 1200 Main Street Indianapolis, Indiana	3,413.00	$ 1,706.43	$ 900.00	$ 806.57	—	—
Allan Sales, Inc. 1413 Liberty Avenue Buffalo, New York	1,312.40	—	1,312.40	—	—	—
Baker Products 19 Gilmore Indus. Drive Pittsburgh, Pa.	784.60	784.60	—	—	—	—
Benson Sports, Inc. 13124 Wilson Blvd. Columbus, Ohio	643.12	41.08	—	102.04	—	500.00 (Dispute)
			— Etc. —			
TOTAL	$78,000.00	$46,412.76	$20,080.40	$7,112.38	$2,200.33	$2,194.13

Exhibit 32

(such as the handling of our checking accounts), and have we followed those recommendations? Should we have a separate payroll acount? What amount of cash should we endeavor to keep in the bank, as a minimum?

ACCOUNTS RECEIVABLE

What does an accounts receivable *aging* (such as in Exhibit 32) look like? If we have such agings for several months, what trends are reflected in these agings? Are there any apparent losses reflected in these agings? Should we establish a reserve for losses? Who serves as Credit Manager? Do we have credit files on each account? Who authorizes the extension of credit, and on what basis? Do we have trade reports on customers? Bank checkings? Do we have credit limits set for each account? Do we have financial statements on larger accounts? Are our receivables records in fire-resistant storage? Do we have a series of collection letters? Who abuses the discount privilege? Do we obtain shipping evidence in all cases? Do we have any customers that we also buy from? How many "days' sales" should we use, as a goal, for accounts receivable? What is the "norm" for our industry?

INVENTORY DETAILS

FINISHED GOODS:
1. Product A, 122 @ $71.25 — $ 8,692.50
2. Product B, 15 @ $908.90 — 13,633.50

— Etc. —

TOTAL — $50,000.00

RAW MATERIALS:
1. Raw steel plate, regular sizes, 33,412 lbs. @ 20¢ — $ 6,682.40
2. Angle iron — 3,700.00
3. Nuts and bolts, standard sizes — 4,857.80

— Etc. —

TOTAL — $46,000.00

WORK IN PROCESS:
1. Product A, 60% finished, 100, @ $42.75 — $ 4,275.00
2. Product B, 50% finished, 6, @ $454.45 — 2,726.70

— Etc. —

TOTAL — $ 9,000.00

Exhibit 33

FIXED ASSET DETAILS

ITEM	SERIAL NO.	CO. NO.	ORIGINAL COST	DATE ACQUIRED	NEW/USED	NET BOOK VALUE	COMMENTS
1. Acme 36″ Bed Model Q Lathe	123479-E	51	$3,429.30	1/20/66	New	$ 3,012.30	On Cond. Sls. Cont.
			— Etc. —				
TOTAL			$178,312.67			$119,600.45	

Exhibit 34

SERIAL DEBT SCHEDULE

CREDITOR	ORIGINAL AMOUNT	CURRENT BALANCE	MONTHLY PAYMENT	COLLATERAL	COMMENT
Acme Machinery	$4,500.00	$ 3,210.40	$ 110.40	Milling Machine, No. 7	Paymts. Cur.
Bystrom Bros., Inc.	2,412.00	1,312.68	78.32	Small lathe, No. 41	Paymts. Cur.
		— Etc. —			
TOTAL		$46,300.00	$ 938.75		

Exhibit 35

			AGING OF
VENDOR	SUPPLIER OF	TOTAL OWING	PURCHASED DECEMBER
Able Products	Rivets	$ 312.40	$ 162.38
Ace Industries, Inc.	Bearings	1,756.90	712.30
Brown Mfg. Co.	Subassemblies	5,026.94	1,100.69
			— Etc. —
TOTAL		$33,000.00	$19,846.20

Exhibit 36

INVENTORY

What did our inventory consist of, the last time we counted it? (See Exhibit 33). What items do we keep on a perpetual inventory, and should we keep more items on that basis, or fewer? Is the inventory adequately but economically insured? When was the last time we reviewed our insurance coverage? Do we have any obsolete or useless goods in our inventory? Who does the purchasing, and is there room for improvement in this function? Do we have alternative sources for all raw materials? Looking ahead, do we have adequate storage space for our finished goods and raw materials inventory? On what basis is the inventory priced? Is the inventory balanced; if not, in what respect is it unbalanced? Do we have too much, or not enough, inventory? How many "Days' Cost of Sales" should we adopt, as an objective? What has our turnover been?

FIXED ASSETS

Review what this item consists of. (See Exhibit 34.) What are the needs for additions, looking ahead? Are there any assets to be disposed of? What is the basis for depreciation? Do we have adequate insurance for these assets? Do we have an organized maintenance program for these assets? A safety program? Conveniently located fire extinguishers? Do we have a facilities layout plan, and if so, where is it? Where are the real estate title documents? Have we had a recent appraisal? Would the estimated "liquidating value" of our machinery be more or less than net book value?

PREPAID AND DEFERRED ITEMS

What does this balance sheet item consist of? Does it include anything that should really be charged off (such as outdated advertising material)?

ACCOUNTS PAYABLE

NOVEMBER	OCTOBER	SEPTEMBER	PRIOR
$ 150.02	—	—	—
812.30	—	$ 34.09	$ 198.21
			(Dispute)
1,412.78	$1,479.80	1,033.67	—
$8,740.11	$3,017.12	$1,174.27	$ 222.30

Exhibit 36 (cont'd)

OTHER ASSETS

What makes up this item?

NOTES PAYABLE—BANK

Are we banking at "the right" bank? What is the current interest rate? Is there a compensating balance requirement? What security have we given for these loans? Is there, or should there be, life insurance assigned in connection with these loans? What is our maximum loan limit at the bank? How often do we send financial statements to the bank? When is our "line" or credit arrangement due for a review by the bank? What do our borrowings look like, from month to month? What are our needs likely to be, looking ahead?

CURRENT MATURITIES AND NOTES AND CONTRACTS, DEFERRED

The details of this type of indebtedness should be detailed more or less as shown in Exhibit 35. If there is any possibility that some of these loans will be repaid with new financing, an approximate payoff figure should be calculated or obtained; frequently, with installment financing, there will be a penalty for prepayment.

ACCOUNTS PAYABLE

What does an aging of our accounts payable look like (Exhibit 36)? Are we taking all discounts? Should we be taking all discounts, or are there some small ones it would be more economical to "ride out" for 30–60 or 90 days? What are the terms we receive from our various suppliers? Do we have creditors who are also customers?

ACCRUALS

What makes up this item on our financial statement? Are our payroll taxes paid to date? Do accruals for wages, vacation pay, etc. look realistic? Are real estate taxes properly accrued?

PROVISION FOR INCOME TAXES

When were we last examined as to income taxes? When did we last review income taxes with our CPA, from the standpoint of tax reduction? Looking ahead, when are the next payments due?

DUE TO OFFICERS

How did these items arise? Are we willing to subrogate or subordinate (delay payment on) these loans or advances to bank credit or other loans? What interest is paid? Have we checked with our CPA regarding the tax implications of this item, and of subordinating this item?

REAL ESTATE MORTGAGE

What is the best guess as to the present value of the land and buildings, and is there room for an increase in the size of the real estate mortgage? If there is room for expansion, would it be possible to obtain the funds for the expansion by redoing the mortgage? What is the interest rate, and is there a penalty clause?

COMMON STOCK, CAPITAL SURPLUS

How many shares are authorized? Outstanding? What is the par value? What are the goals of the stockholders in the long run? Have we ever computed book values and earnings on a *per share* basis? Would it make sense to make such calculations, and then to "price" the stock at a multiple of earnings to see what the theoretical "public stock issue" value might be?

EARNED SURPLUS

What are the profit goals, looking ahead? Is there any problem on income taxes because of the accumulation of earned surplus? What has the dividend policy and thinking been, and what is it, looking ahead?

Matching these thoughts with our previous "where have we been" thinking, now you are ready to look ahead. . . .

7

Where Do We Want to Go?

—MONTAIGNE, as quoted on page 185 of
The Practical Cogitator,
Houghton Mifflin Co., 1945

LOOKING BACK OVER THE RECORD OF "WHERE WE HAVE BEEN," ideas about where we are "drifting" emerge. Trends in various sets of figures suggest that the business is headed in a particular direction in one respect or another, and if an outsider—someone not intimately familiar with the business—were to be asked about the direction the business is heading, he would likely rely on the simple projection of such trends as are apparent in the figures. But, although one certainly cannot ignore trends apparent in the various figures and statistics that describe the past progress of the business, it is a mistake to think that a projection, in the best sense, consists of simply projecting such trends.

Actually, what happens in the future depends more on what management *does* in the future than on anything else, and management—sometimes precisely because it wants to reverse certain trends that have become apparent—may plan on doing things not at all suggested by past trends and records. It might be fair to say, however, that management should—before going ahead with a full-scale projection of its plans—think hard about where the apparent trends do point. After all, there is the implication that, if things just continue as in the past, the business will drift along in the pattern indicated. In the business we have been studying, for example, we have seen that, if things continue as they appear to be trending, working capital is going to develop in an unfavorable way, and that the need for short-term bank credit will continue to increase. Since the worse the working capital picture looks the more difficult it is likely to be to borrow money at the bank, these two trends really point toward trouble. This is the type of observation that management should make, concerning the past and the trends apparent in past figures, before it sets down even the broad dimensions of a projection designed to translate its actual desires for the future to black-and-white figures.

Dreams are another important ingredient for projections. Yes, the hopes and dreams of top management for the future of its business must be incorporated in any meaningful projection of the firm's future, even though they may become altered as they are matched up with realistic facts about the past, the present, and the future in the projection process.

Particularly at the outset, as it begins to get seriously down to business in doing its planning, it is important for management to think broadly, in large and comprehensive terms. For example, does it really want the business to grow—or to grow gradually, or rapidly? Recognizing that growth will make new demands on the physical resources, the personnel and the management of the business, is management really committed to meeting these new demands? Is management, or management-ownership, *enjoying* the development of the business; or, would it make management happier if it were possible to liquidate the investment it has in the business and place the funds in another type of investment entirely? If there is ever a proper time to dig down and ask such basic questions, it is in preparation for a projection into the future of management's plans.

In broad terms, the management of the company which is described by the figures we are using, decided this: that it is desirable for the company to grow as rapidly as possible, and that one of the prime reasons for preparing a projection is to see how rapidly the company *can* grow; that is, the projection should reflect such problems as will arise from growth. Then management will be in a position to intelligently tackle these various problems, ranging perhaps from obtaining additional financing to major changes in the physical plant and in the personnel and organizational arrangements as they now exist.

Having taken a peek at the future in terms of "trends we are drifting with" and having put the feet up on the desk to dream a bit and ask some really basic questions about the future, now we are in a position to describe in more detail the type of projection we want to prepare.

If one word could be used to describe the most important characteristic of a really good projection, that word would be *realistic*. Why? Because the point of the entire effort is not to persuade or impress anyone; the point is to form as accurate a picture as possible of what the future holds for the business—and such a picture will not emerge if the various input factors are weighted either too optimistically or too pessimistically.

For example, if sales are projected on a basis that is too optimistic, the projection will wind up "saying" that there are accounts receivable to be carried and inventory to be carried, and therefore financial needs that may never occur, and thus paint a financial picture that is too pessimistic. On the other hand, a relatively pessimistic sales projection may *understate* the financial need, and thus be too optimistic from the financial angle. This is why it is not at all unusual to prepare *three* versions of a projection: one that is on the optimistic side as concerns operations (sales), one that is pessimistic, and one that is "middle of the road."

Here, for the purpose of illustration, we will prepare just one version of a projection, as is indeed the customary thing to do. However, it should be kept in mind that it is possible to exaggerate various aspects of the business picture by being either too optimistic or too pessimistic, and that once the projection is finished, it may be well to go back and redo it with another set of assumptions—the better to see and understand the resulting problems and opportunities.

But enough of generalities; it is now time to begin the actual projection process.

8
Getting the Future
Down on Paper

Develop your report so that it can be read with comprehension in the future as well as today. Reports are useful in determining immediate policies, but they should also be useful for later reference. Hence make all statements so complete and exact that the report will be useful to an executive or investigator who picks it up years later.

—Page 10, *Report Writing,*
by Guam, Graves, and Hoffman,
Prentice-Hall, Inc., 1949 ed.

So far it is clear that we are going to prepare some kind of projection, one that might be described as aggressive (we want to grow) and realistic (we want to know what the problems are going to be). But just how do you go about this; where do you start?

Where you start may depend on the stance or posture of the business. For example, if the company is in the enviable position of being sure that it can sell all of the product it can make, why then, of course, you would begin with *production,* because that will be the primary determinant in the future. In our case, however, although the sales picture is bright it isn't quite that bright, so management decides to start with *sales,* because it is the sales function that begins the cycle of SALES/ ACCOUNTS RECEIVABLE/CASH/INVENTORY/FINISHED GOODS INVENTORY/SALES/etc., etc. . . .

Thus the first part of the projection, dealt with in detail in the next chapter, has to do with *sales*. Once decisions have been made regarding the projected level of sales, attention will next turn to *costs,* and *gross profits.* Next will come *expenses,* and finally *net profits.* Once all those elements have been considered, there will emerge a projected profit and loss statement—in effect a statement that "here is what is *going* to happen, in terms of operations."

Then, with operations spread out in a projected fashion, the next question that arises is, "OK, let us assume this kind of operations picture; *if* it is achieved, what will the *cash flow* be; how will the money flow in and out?" This part of the projection must be pursued in just as much detail, and just as carefully, as the P. & L. statement.

Finally, assuming that operations develop as projected, and that the cash flows in and out in certain ways, "So what?" Where does all this leave us? The answers are provided by pro forma balance sheets, which reflect "where we will *be*" if all of the assumptions that have gone into the P. & L. statement and the cash flow exhibits are accurate. In other words, assuming certain sales, costs, and expenses, and a certain pattern of cash flow, here are the results as they would appear—or, here are the problems!

At each point in the projection, there will be detailed figures to work with, to reduce to totals or subtotals. It is important that all of the details be preserved and that the details are laid out in a manner that facilitates reference to them.

Footnotes—detailed comments that explain the reasoning or the assumptions that were involved when the estimate was prepared—should be made in all cases, so that the various exhibits are meaningful documents, and not just "scratch pads" which lose all significance once the "answer" is determined. If such details of the thinking that lies behind the projection are preserved, the finished documents can then serve important functions aside from simply supplying answers to such questions as to how much money must be borrowed. Each schedule involved in the projection can be a "road map" for a particular part of the business, once the overall projection or some version of it is adopted as an operating plan.

9
Sales

A salesman who is told to go out and sell as much as he can rarely equals the production of the man who has a definite daily objective to see ten prospects, sell two units, or bring in $200 worth of orders. A salesman not only works harder but also works more happily when he knows what is expected of him. In addition to providing a fixed task, sales quotas afford numerous advantages:

1. *They provide convenient measuring sticks to determine the comparative value of various salesmen.*
2. *They facilitate the coordination of production and sales.*
3. *They provide a basis for salesmen's compensation plans, particularly bonus systems.*
4. *They serve as a basis for sales budgets.*
5. *They provide incentive to salesmen to increase efforts.*
6. *They enable the proper distribution of advertising, warehouse stocks, and manpower.*
7. *They increase efficiency of the distributing system.*

—Page 429, *Sales Administration Principles and Problems,*
by BERTRAND R. CANFIELD,
Prentice-Hall, Inc., 1947

GROSS SALES

JUST TO BE ABSOLUTELY CLEAR ABOUT THE MATTER: HERE WE ARE talking about the sales dollars *before* any deduction, such as for goods returned, or for discounts allowed; those and any similar factors will be allowed for, later, as a separate function.

VARIOUS METHODS OF ESTIMATING

Perhaps the easiest way to estimate sales would be to go to a graph or chart showing what sales have been, and then simply place an "X" where it looks as though it "belongs." But, although this procedure would be fairly simple, it would be useless. If the projection is worth doing at all, the calculation of perhaps the most important single set of figures in the projection—the sales figures—certainly deserves more thought than that. And, if the projection is to be used to persuade a banker or impress an investor—think beyond the "easy X."

Here are several different means of making an *educated* guess as to what sales will be:

Unit Sales: If a business manufactures a line of products, often the best way to come up with a good estimate of future sales is to begin with an analysis of what has been sold in the past, in terms of numbers of units. For example, if a factory produces three kinds of products or units, it is almost certain that these are showing different trends. By estimating future sales for each product or type of unit on a unit basis, first, then multiplying the unit sales projection by a dollar value, to get estimated dollar sales, there is more logic behind the dollar totals resulting. This approach is also particularly useful where there are different seasonal factors involved in some products or units. In such cases it could be practical to arrive at a monthly sales estimate, in dollars, by adding together several separately determined dollar sales estimates by different products, with a separate schedule setting forth the number of units per month, the unit sales prices assumed, and the resulting totals.

By Salesman: Assuming you have ten salesmen, an estimate from each of them, together with an estimate for house accounts, etc., will add up to a total sales estimate. They may be asked to estimate in terms of units or in terms of dollars, depending on which basis you believe they are best able to project. The unit approach is really preferable, because it is product you want to sell, and the dollars are simply what results by multiplying the units by sales prices. In any event, the opinions and the feelings of your salesmen about future prospects are important, and it is necessary to reflect their thinking in the projection in some manner.

By Area: In some cases using areas for sales estimates may amount to the same thing as using salesmen, but in other cases the area figures may have more application. For example, there is data available on various areas which may make it possible for you to project that you will sell so much product in certain states, counties, metropolitan areas, or other area breakdowns, in which case the area approach could be a valid one. If "Area A—$40,000" makes sense in your business, use this approach, either as the primary basis for an estimate or as a supplementary approach; often by using two or three different approaches the best answer emerges.

Key Accounts: An example of a situation where you would use projections for "key accounts" is that of the manufacturer who produces goods either exclusively or principally for "private label" distribution. In such a situation you would, perhaps, think in terms of *units per customer,* but not in terms of salesmen or areas. But even if you have only three or four key accounts, out of hundreds, it may be well to cross-check your thinking by preparing estimates for your "key accounts."

Production: Occasionally this whole job is greatly simplified because a company is in the enviable position of having a practically unlimited demand for its product in the forseeable future, and therefore sales really *are* dependent on the production capacity. In such a case, it makes a lot of sense to first dig deep into matters of production capacity. Even in other situations, it is well to think through your sales estimates in terms of your capacity to produce, so that you will be able to say something like, "at this level we are predicting, our production is about two-thirds of capacity."

Degree of Market Penetration: In some cases, a company may have rather precise information on the total sales of its type of product in a given area, and be able to say rather accurately just what part of the total market it has enjoyed in previous periods, and what part of the market can reasonably be expected in the future. Thus, in some cases it might make sense to base the projection of sales on a total market of so much, *"x%"* of which the company expects to get. Even if sales are estimated in an entirely different manner, and on a completely different basis, it would be well to have at least an approximate idea of what the total market picture is, and how your company is faring in that market.

Company's First Attempt

After considering the various alternatives, in this particular instance management decided that its best bet might be to try and predict an annual sales volume for each of its *products*. It went back five years and analyzed the breakdown of its sales into five different product areas, in addition to service and miscellaneous sales. The information was first obtained some time ago, when the company was simply analyzing all of the data it had available; this is now shown in Exhibit 37.

ANALYSIS AND PROJECTION—SALES—BY PRODUCT

	YEAR 1	YEAR 2	YEAR 3	YEAR 4	YEAR 5	FIRST TRY PROJECTED YEAR 6
Product A	$100,000	$110,000	$120,000	$130,000	$140,000	$150,000
B	——	70,000	85,000	100,000	90,000	80,000
C	——	15,000	90,000	140,000	145,000	150,000
D	——	——	——	20,000	100,000	300,000
E	——	——	——	——	15,000	150,000
Service	——	2,000	3,000	5,000	8,000	15,000
Misc.	——	3,000	2,000	5,000	2,000	5,000
	$100,000	$200,000	$300,000	$400,000	$500,000	$850,000

Exhibit 37

In this first attempt, it would be noted that the company came up with a substantial increase over the previous year: $350,000 on top of $500,000 for the past year, for a total of $850,000. Because of the significance of the amount of increase, management decided that it would have to look over this estimate more carefully before it could settle on such a figure. Such consideration led to the next step.

Second Approach

Next the company decided to go to its salesmen with the problem of projecting an annual sales volume, and see what their thoughts might be. Each salesman was first provided with data about the past, showing how much of each product he had sold in his particular area of responsibility for each of the preceding five years. The salesmen were asked to study the information concerning the past, and with their knowledge regarding the product line of the company presently, to make a projection regarding their estimated sales for the coming year.

It was first made clear to them that the company had aggressive plans for the coming year and that in all likelihood they would be receiving higher quotas and should be as realistic as possible as to their estimates, because management was approaching the proposition of projecting sales from several different aspects. Moreover, any salesman who could not carry his weight in the aggressive new program would be in trouble anyway.

In addition to the estimates from present salesmen, management prepared an estimate for a new salesman whose area would be mostly new to the company. Management also completed an estimate of house accounts and sales to be made by agents, as well as a small miscellaneous category. The results of the various estimates are shown in Exhibit 38, together with comparable data for the past five years.

ANALYSIS AND PROJECTION—SALES BY SALESMAN

	YEAR 1	YEAR 2	YEAR 3	YEAR 4	YEAR 5	PROJECTED YEAR 6
Salesman Smith	$100,000	$ 60,000	$ 40,000	$130,000	$150,000	$200,000
Salesman Jones	——	100,000	205,000	180,000	250,000	300,000
New Salesman	——	——	——	——	——	150,000[b]
"House Accounts"	——	40,000	30,000	40,000	42,000	50,000
Agents	——	——	20,000	35,000	50,000	100,000
Misc.[a]	——	——	5,000	15,000	8,000	10,000
TOTAL	$100,000	$200,000	$300,000	$400,000	$500,000	$810,000

[a]Incomplete records made a "plug" necessary.
[b]New salesman not yet hired; estimate made by management.

Exhibit 38

The first thing to be noted is that the total estimated sales for the next year came to $810,000, or $40,000 less than the estimate first determined by management, using product lines only as a method of prediction.

SECOND TRY, ANALYSIS AND PROJECTION—SALES—BY PRODUCT

	YEAR 1	YEAR 2	YEAR 3	YEAR 4	YEAR 5	1ST TRY PROJECTED YEAR 6	2D TRY PROJECTED YEAR 6
Product A	$100,000	$110,000	$120,000	$130,000	$140,000	$150,000	$150,000
B	——	70,000	85,000	100,000	90,000	80,000	80,000
C	——	15,000	90,000	140,000	145,000	150,000	150,000
D	——	——	——	20,000	100,000	300,000	270,000
E	——	——	——	——	15,000	150,000	140,000
Service	——	2,000	3,000	5,000	8,000	15,000	15,000
Misc.	——	3,000	2,000	5,000	2,000	5,000	5,000
TOTAL	$100,000	$200,000	$300,000	$400,000	$500,000	$850,000	$810,000

Exhibit 39

PROJECTION—SALES BY MONTHS

YEAR	JAN.	FEB.	MAR.	APRIL	MAY	JUNE	JULY	AUG.	SEPT.	OCT.	NOV.	DEC.	TOTAL
1	5%	10%	7%	7%	9%	5%	10%	12%	8%	6%	10%	11%	100%
2	4½	6½	5	5½	7	9	6½	9½	10½	13½	16	6½	100
3	8½	9½	11½	9	8½	10	6½	5	9½	3½	9	9½	100
4	7½	7½	9	5½	7½	5½	9½	10	11	9	7½	10½	100
5	7½	8	8½	5	7	6½	8	11	9½	9½	9½	10	100
TOTAL	33	41½	41	32	39	36	40½	47½	48½	41½	52	47½	500
Average	6.6%	8.3%	8.2%	6.4%	7.8%	7.2%	8.1%	9.5%	9.7%	8.3%	10.4%	9.5%	100%
Projected Year 6%	7	8	8	5	6	7	8	9	11	10	11	10	100
Projected Year 6 $	57,000	65,000	65,000	41,000	49,000	57,000	65,000	73,000	88,000	81,000	88,000	81,000	810,000

Exhibit 40

Third Approach

Having two different previous estimates, determined really in two different ways, management next gave a thorough reconsideration to each. It was decided that the analysis by product would be reviewed again, to see if it could be brought in line with the salesmen's estimates. This second attempt, purposely made to come out to $810,000 (which was the estimate the salesmen came up with), is shown in Exhibit 39.

Although it is not reflected in any Exhibit contained here, obviously management would make most careful comparisons between the product sales estimates prepared by the salesmen (that is, how much of each product each salesman thought he would sell), and the management guess by product line. Here we assume that there was very good correlation, because management decided to use as an estimate for its next year's sales $810,000.

THE TIMING OF SALES

Next management turned its attention to the problem of allocating the yearly sales figure over the year; that is, deciding how much sales would be for each month. In order to review this subject, management went back to an analysis that was made at an earlier stage in the preparation of material for the projection, and looked at Exhibit 14. Then, it reviewed with salesmen their individual estimates by months and ultimately arrived at a division calculated by allocating a certain percent of total yearly sales to each month, as reflected in Exhibit 40.

This type of data is often best observed by charting the various figures, and the graph shown in Exhibit 41 shows what the sales curve looked like for the past five years, and also what the year ahead would look like, as projected.

RETURNS AND ALLOWANCES

With a gross sales figure for each month during the coming year, management now had the ability to fill in the first line on the profit and loss statement projection: gross sales. Next, attention turned to the second item on the projected P. & L. statement: returns and allowances.

Management discussed this matter at some length and studied the data contained in Exhibit 17, which had been developed earlier. It concluded that it would be reasonable to assume that returns and allowances would average 1 percent of gross sales in the coming year, and since the gross sales figure was already available, this gave management the ability to determine a returns and allowances figure for each month during the coming year.

NET SALES

Since net sales is the difference between gross sales and returns and allowances, and management has already arrived at monthly estimates for both of these items, it also has the ability to enter net sales on their projection form; so the first three items on the projection form are now complete (See Exhibit 42).

Next, we proceed to the Cost of Goods Sold section of the Profit and Loss Statement, covered in the next chapter.

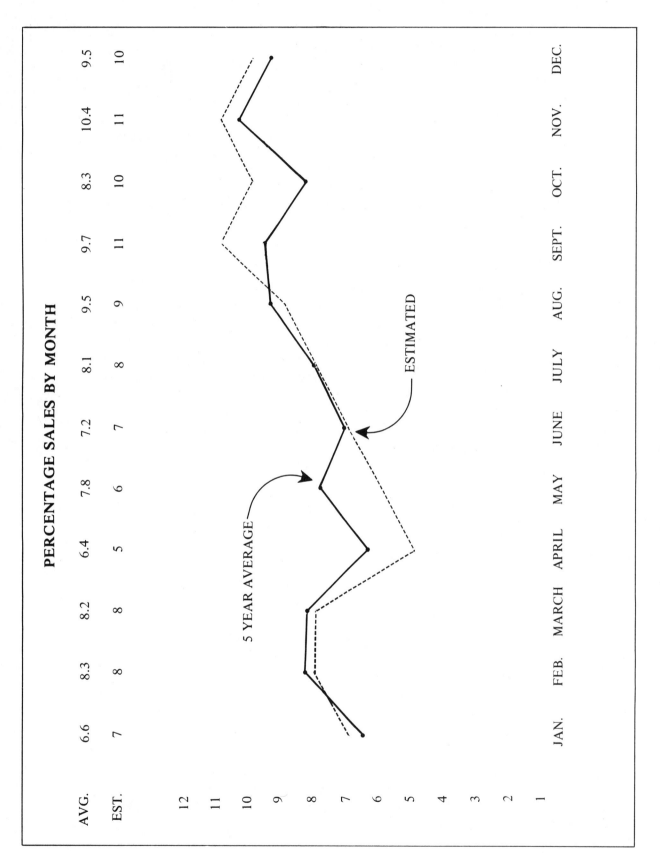

PERCENTAGE SALES BY MONTH

| AVG. | 6.6 | 8.3 | 8.2 | 6.4 | 7.8 | 7.2 | 8.1 | 9.5 | 9.7 | 8.3 | 10.4 | 9.5 |
| EST. | 7 | 8 | 8 | 5 | 6 | 7 | 8 | 9 | 11 | 10 | 11 | 10 |

5 YEAR AVERAGE

ESTIMATED

| JAN. | FEB. | MARCH | APRIL | MAY | JUNE | JULY | AUG. | SEPT. | OCT. | NOV. | DEC. |

Exhibit 41

PROJECTED PROFIT AND LOSS STATEMENT (THROUGH NET SALES)

	JAN.	FEB.	MARCH	APRIL	MAY	JUNE	JULY	AUG.	SEPT.	OCT.	NOV.	DEC.	TOTAL
GROSS SALES	57,000	65,000	65,000	41,000	49,000	57,000	65,000	73,000	88,000	81,000	88,000	81,000	810,000
(Less: Returns & Allow.)	(570)	(650)	(650)	(410)	(490)	(670)	(650)	(730)	(880)	(810)	(880)	(810)	(8,100)
NET SALES	56,430	64,350	64,350	40,590	48,510	56,430	64,350	72,270	87,120	80,190	87,120	80,190	801,900

COST OF GOODS SOLD:

Cost of Goods Mfg'd:

Beg. Inv., WIP
(Less End. Inv., WIP)
Change, WIP *

Beg. Inv., Raw Mat'l.
Purchases
Goods Available
(Less End. Inv., R. M.) *
Materials Used *
Labor Used *
Manufacturing Expenses *
TOTAL, C. OF G. M. *

Cost of Goods Sold:

Beg. Inv., Fin. Gds.
Cost of Gds. Mfg'd.
Goods Available
(Less End. Inv., F. Gds.)
TOTAL, C. OF G. S.

GROSS PROFIT

EXPENSES:

Sales Expense
Gen'l. & Admin. Expense
TOTAL EXPENSES

OPERATING PROFIT

OTHER INCOME (OTHER CHARGES)—NET

PROFIT BEFORE INCOME TAXES

PROVISION FOR INCOME TAXES

PROFIT AFTER INCOME TAXES

Exhibit 42

59

10
Cost of Goods Sold

As applied to ideation, the oft-used term of synthesis is inadequate. Even the act of bringing things together into new combinations may take more than synthesis alone. Often it calls for breaking a problem into separate parts and then regrouping them. Analyzing, hunting, and combining and otherwise changing—these are all parts of creative research. Scientific experimentation calls into play all of these activities and more.

> —page 35, *Applied Imagination,*
> by ALEX F. OSBORN,
> Charles Scribner's Sons, 1957

THE GENERAL FORMULA FOR DETERMINING COST OF GOODS SOLD IS AS follows:

$$
\begin{aligned}
&\ \text{Beginning Inventory} \\
&+\ \text{Purchases} \\
&=\ \text{Subtotal} \\
&-\ \text{(Ending Inventory)} \\
&=\ \text{Cost of Goods Sold}
\end{aligned}
$$

In preparing the forecast we are, as mentioned several times previously, always working from the *known* to the *unknown*. In this formula, you might know the beginning inventory, the purchases, and the ending inventory, in which case you are in a position to figure the cost of goods sold. On the other hand, you might know the beginning inventory and the purchases, and have some idea of what the cost of goods sold is, but not know the ending inventory. In such a case, it is necessary to "turn the formula around" to arrive at the desired figure.

To illustrate, let us assign values to the various items in the formula:

	Beginning Inventory	$200.00
+	Purchases	$400.00
=	Subtotal	$600.00
−	(Ending Inventory)	($150.00)
=	Cost of Goods Sold	$450.00

In looking at the above figures, it is easy to see that the purchases, added to the beginning inventory, give a subtotal which could be called "goods available for sale." Further, when one subtracts what is left (the ending inventory) from the subtotal, the resultant figure is cost of goods sold.

Very frequently, and generally in connection with the preparation of interim financial statements, the ending inventory is *not* known. Therefore, it is estimated, usually on the basis of estimating the cost of goods sold to be a certain percentage of sales.

For example, if one assumes that the cost of goods sold is 80 percent or the gross profit is 20 percent, by twisting around the formula, one can determine what the ending inventory should be. To give an illustration:

	Beginning Inventory	$200.00
+	Purchases	$400.00
=	Subtotal	$600.00
−	(Cost of Goods Sold)	($450.00)
=	Ending Inventory	$150.00

You will note that in using the above "changed around formula," we really moved from knowns to unknowns by saying in effect that we start with a certain inventory figure, to which we add purchases of a certain amount, which gives us the goods to be accounted for; next, we take out of the goods to be accounted for an estimate for the goods that were removed in the process of sales, and this leaves us with an ending inventory figure which is an estimate.

This process of working from known to unknown factors is very important to grasp, so other illustrations will be given here. For example, let us suppose that you know what your beginning inventory is and you know what your desired inventory levels are, but you are wondering how much you are going to have to buy or what purchases might amount to. In such a case, you might arrange the formula as follows:

	Beginning Inventory	$200.00	
−	(Cost of Goods Sold)	($450.00)	
=	Ending Inventory	($250.00)	(if no purchases)
+	Desired Ending Inventory	$150.00	
	Purchases	$400.00	

In the above illustration, we start out knowing what we had in inventory, and we remove from that inventory the items that will be sold, at their cost value. This tells us what kind of inventory position would be left if we let the sales go out and didn't buy anything at all. In the above case, we would have a *deficit* inventory of $250.00. Next, we show below that figure in our formula the *desired* ending inventory of $150.00, and the remaining figure (purchases) is determined by seeing what amount of purchases it would take to cover the inventory deficit and leave an ending inventory of $150.00.

Just to stretch the imagination, it is also possible that a person might be in a position of knowing what the *ending* inventory is and not knowing what the *beginning* inventory was, and having a need to find out. In such a case, the formula can again be "twisted" to yield an answer. For example:

	Ending Inventory	$150.00
+	Cost of Goods Sold	$450.00
=	Subtotal	$600.00
−	Purchases	($400.00)
	Beginning Inventory	$200.00

As can be seen above, the reasoning proceeded as follows: we had $150.00 at the end of the operation, and sold $450.00 at cost, which means that we had $600.00 thereafter to be accounted for. Of the $600.00 we have records of having purchased $400.00 worth, so the beginning inventory must have been $200.00.

Calculating the cost of goods sold for any company will utilize reasoning such as outlined above. However, it is really much simpler to compute the cost of goods sold, the related gross profits, and the related movements in inventory and purchases, for a *trading* company than it is for a manufacturing company. A manufacturer must be concerned not only with what he is selling, but also with what he is producing. It is not simply a question of how much goods come in and out of the warehouse. For this reason, we have elected in this book to explain the more complex methodology, because if you can follow it, you will have no trouble with the simpler problems. Also, since our case history is that of a manufacturer, to be consistent we must work along with the problems that confront this particular company.

COST OF GOODS MANUFACTURED

A manufacturer must first determine what it is costing him to *produce* goods, before he can determine what it is costing him to *sell* goods.

The format for a profit and loss statement for a manufacturing concern is, therefore, somewhat different from that for a trading concern. To illustrate, a typical P. & L. statement for a manufacturer, insofar as the cost of goods sold section is concerned, would consist of the following headings:

Cost of Goods Sold:
    Cost of Goods Manufactured:
        Beginning Inventory, Work in Process
      + Materials Purchased
      + Labor Expended

+ Manufacturing Expenses
− Ending Inventory, Work in Process

The above formula will tell a manufacturer what it is costing him to manufacture goods; to go one step further, and find out what it is costing him to sell goods, he must use the following formula:

Beginning Inventory, Finished Goods
+ Cost of Goods Manufactured
= Subtotal
− Ending Inventory, Finished Goods
= Cost of Goods Sold

This formula is, in general, the one that we must work with in this particular case, since the company we are working with is a manufacturing concern.

WORK-IN-PROCESS INVENTORY

Since the first item in the formula is work in process, this is what we must deal with first in making an estimate for our company.

Our first step is to examine the *knowns* of the situation. It seemed reasonable, first, to study the relationship between gross sales activity in the past and work-in-process inventory. This was done, as is shown in Exhibit 43, and then production people were invited to discuss this subject. They felt strongly that since the company was talking about producing on the basis of almost double the amount of sales volume, that the work-in-process inventory figure should rise during the year, so that by the year end it would be at least $27,000.00. The "turn" of inventory was also considered. This matter received considerable attention and finally it was decided that a work-in-process inventory which would show a gradual increase would be used, with $27,000.00 being the figure at the end of the year. The change in the beginning and ending in-

RELATIONSHIPS, *WIP* INVENTORY AND GROSS SALES

YEAR	GROSS SALES	WIP INVENTORY	WIP AS % OF SALES
1	100,000	9,000	9.0%
2	200,000	5,000	2.5
3	300,000	8,000	2.7
4	400,000	14,000	3.5
5	500,000	9,000	1.8
6	900,000[a]	27,000	3.0

[a]Year 6 *production,* expressed in sales dollars.

Exhibit 43

SCHEDULE, CHANGES IN *W/P* INVENTORY

	JAN.	FEB.	MAR.	APR.	MAY	JUNE	JULY	AUG.	SEPT.	OCT.	NOV.	DEC.
Beg. Inv.	9,000[a]	10,500	12,000	13,500	15,000	16,500	18,000	19,500	21,000	22,500	24,000	25,500
End. Inv.	10,500	12,000	13,500	15,000	16,500	18,000	19,500	21,000	22,500	24,000	25,500	27,000
Change[b]	1,500	1,500	1,500	1,500	1,500	1,500	1,500	1,500	1,500	1,500	1,500	1,500

[a]Balance at end of December.
[b]Increase of $18,000 (from $9,000 to $27,000) would average out to an increase of $1,500 per month, which estimate was used.

Exhibit 44

ventory for each month, for work-in-process, was worked out in Exhibit 44. As is shown in that Exhibit, an average change of $1,500.00 per month would take the beginning inventory of work-in-process up from $9,000 to $27,000 by the end of the year. Production management seemed satisfied with this estimate, and therefore it was adopted.

Now, we are able to fill in another part of the P. & L. statement. Just to keep our thinking straight, and to see how we move along, take a look at Exhibit 45, and note that we have cleared up the sales, net sales, and work-in-process sections of the P. & L. statement. Next, it appears that we will have to tackle the matter of raw materials, purchases, and related inventories.

MATERIAL COSTS

It is necessary to talk very specifically about products and particular lines of goods in order to discuss material costs. In this case, the company broke it down by product. Every manufacturing concern has, or should have, a "bill of materials" for every item that it manufactures, showing what goes into the goods in terms of materials.

As shown on Exhibit 46, the company first took a per-unit material cost, and determined what percentage the material ran to selling price. Next, it estimated a volume of production product by product, in keeping with the overall management decision as to what would be produced and sold, and applied this percentage to the production figure (expressed in terms of sales dollars) so as to arrive at an estimated material cost for the goods that were actually to be produced during the period.

TIMING OF PRODUCTION

The next question that arises in connection with production is *when*. That is, assuming that so many goods must be produced during a period, exactly on what day must they be produced and during what week and during what month.

As shown in Exhibit 47, first the "curve" of sales was examined, and next an absolutely equal production figure for every month was examined. Then, with these two sets of figures in front of them, and all the other facts they know about the production process in mind, the production people determined a production curve. This curve gave effect to the fact that in July and August many employees took a vacation, and therefore production would be less. It also illustrated the fact that the company would be pushing harder toward the end of the year and therefore October and November efforts would be heavier than normal.

Next, the production percentage that was decided upon was applied to the material purchases. As shown on Exhibit 48, this means that, of the total of $334,800.00 worth of materials to be used during the period, 7 percent would be used during the month of January because this is the estimated amount of production that would take place then.

Next, as shown on Exhibit 49, the "known" information regarding raw materials was placed on a work sheet. As reflected in the Exhibit, this gives effect to the fact

PROJECTED PROFIT AND LOSS STATEMENT

		JAN.	FEB.	MAR.	APR.	MAY
GROSS SALES		57,000	65,000	65,000	41,000	49,000
(Less: Returns & Allow.)		(570)	(650)	(650)	(410)	(490)
NET SALES		56,430	64,350	64,350	40,590	48,510
COST OF GOODS SOLD:						
Cost of Goods Mfg'd.:						
Beg. Inv., WIP		9,000	10,500	12,000	13,500	15,000
(Less End. Inv., WIP)		(10,500)	(12,000)	(13,500)	(15,000)	(16,500)
Change, WIP	*	(1,500)	(1,500)	(1,500)	(1,500)	(1,500)
Beg. Inv., Raw Mat'l.						
Purchases						
Goods Available						
(Less End. Inv., R. M.)						
Materials Used	*					
Labor Used	*					
Manufacturing Expenses	*					
TOTAL, C. OF G. M.	*					
Cost of Goods Sold:						
Beg. Inv., Fin. Gds.						
Cost of Gds. Mfg'd.						
Goods, Available						
(Less End. Inv., F. Gds.)						
TOTAL, C. OF G. S.						
GROSS PROFIT						
EXPENSES:						
Sales Expense						
Gen'l. & Admin. Expense						
TOTAL EXPENSES						
OPERATING PROFIT						
OTHER INCOME (OTHER CHARGES)—NET						
PROFIT BEFORE INCOME TAXES						
PROVISION FOR INCOME TAXES						
PROFIT AFTER INCOME TAXES						

Exhibit 45

that we know the beginning inventory figure is $46,000.00. It also shows the estimated usage for each of the 12 months, and shows the total of that usage. Next, you will note that it shows what the ending inventory would be if there should be *no* purchases. Here we are taking, once again, a basic formula (beginning inventory plus purchases, minus usage, equals ending inventory) and "twisting" it around to suit our purposes. Thus Exhibit 49 leaves a line on which purchases can be placed and also reflects still

(THROUGH *WIP* INVENTORY)

JUNE	JULY	AUG.	SEPT.	OCT.	NOV.	DEC.	TOTAL
57,000	65,000	73,000	88,000	81,000	88,000	81,000	810,000
(570)	(650)	(730)	(880)	(810)	(880)	(810)	(8,100)
56,430	64,350	72,270	87,120	80,190	87,120	80,190	801,900
16,500	18,000	19,500	21,000	22,500	24,000	25,500	9,000
(18,000)	(19,500)	(21,000)	(22,500)	(24,000)	(25,500)	(27,000)	(27,000)
(1,500)	(1,500)	(1,500)	(1,500)	(1,500)	(1,500)	(1,500)	(18,000)

Exhibit 45 (cont'd)

one more decision, concerning ending inventory. An ending inventory of $83,000.00 was estimated on the basis of an 80 percent increase, or $900,000.00 of production versus $500,000.00 of sales last year.

Next, a little more formula "twisting" was utilized to determine the amount of purchases. As reflected in a footnote to Exhibit 49, the ending inventory and beginning inventory were compared and it was noted that a $37,000.00 increase

ESTIMATED MATERIAL COSTS

	A UNIT SALES PRICE	B EST. UNIT MATERIAL COST	C MATERIAL AS % OF SALES (B DIV. A)	D EST. VOLUME OF PRODUC.[a]	E EST. MATERIAL COSTS (C × D)
Product A	$500.00	$187.00	37.4%	$160,000	$ 59,880
B	200.00	76.00	38.0	85,000	32,300
C	500.00	200.00	40.0	155,000	62,000
D	600.00	213.60	35.6	320,000	113,920
E	300.00	111.00	37.0	160,000	59,200
Service	——	——	40.0[b]	15,000	6,000
Misc.	——	——	30.0[b]	5,000	1,500
		TOTAL		$900,000	$334,800

[a] In terms of sales dollars.
[b] Arbitrary estimate.

Exhibit 46

PRODUCTION TIMING

	SALES		"EQUAL"		"PRODUCTION"	
	MO.	CUM.	MO.	CUM.	MO.	CUM.
January	7%	7%	8.33%	8.33%	7%	7%
February	8	15	"	16.66	8	15
March	8	23	"	24.99	8	23
April	5	28	"	33.32	9	32
May	6	34	"	41.65	9	41
June	7	41	"	49.98	10	51
July	8	49	"	58.31	6	57
August	9	58	"	66.64	6	63
September	11	69	"	74.97	9	72
October	10	79	"	83.30	10	82
November	11	90	"	91.63	10	92
December	10	100	"	99.99	8	100
TOTAL	100%		100%		100%	

Exhibit 47

would take place; in addition, there would be a usage of $334,800.00, which tells us that total purchases would be $371,800.00. Then, logically, the next step is to find out *when* the purchases will take place.

In order to determine the timing of purchases, attention was given to the matter

ESTIMATED MATERIAL USAGE

	PRODUCTION PERCENTAGE	MATERIAL USAGE
January	7%	$ 23,436
February	8	26,784
March	8	26,784
April	9	30,132
May	9	30,132
June	10	33,480
July	6	20,088
August	6	20,088
September	9	30,132
October	10	33,480
November	10	33,480
December	8	26,784
	100%	$334,800

Exhibit 48

of the production "curve" and the timing of material purchases. As shown on Exhibit 50, a one-month lead time was determined to be the best approximation of how the system should work. For example, in February 8 percent of the production activity for the year was to take place, so 8 percent of the materials to be ordered for the year should be ordered so as to be received in January. Likewise, since the figure for March was 8 percent, the February purchases would be 8 percent, the purchases rising to 9 percent in March because the April production is scheduled for 9 percent. And so on, down to November at which time the one month lead approach no longer works. Therefore, the December figure for purchases was simply a "plug" figure to account for a total of 100 percent. As reflected in this same Exhibit, the percentages for purchases, with one month lead time, were then applied to the total purchase figure of $371,800.00, to yield a monthly purchase figure. Exhibit 51 shows what the raw materials work sheet looks like when this new information is inserted.

All that remains, then, to determine the beginning and ending inventory for raw materials is to complete the chart, a mathematical process. The end result is shown in Exhibit 52. Finally, from the raw materials work sheet we are able to post to our evolving P. & L. statement the information relating to raw materials. The P. & L. statement as it appears once this information is posted is shown in Exhibit 53. It is noted from looking at that Exhibit the next item to merit attention is labor.

LABOR

Using much the same logic as was used in determining material costs (that is, going back to individual product units, and determining the estimated unit labor cost, and relating this to the selling price), the total labor required for $900,000.00

RAW MATERIALS (THROUGH USAGE)

	JAN.	FEB.	MAR.	APR.	MAY	JUNE	JULY	AUG.	SEPT.	OCT.	NOV.	DEC.	TOTAL	"PROOF"
Beg. Inv.	46,000ᵃ													46,000ᵃ
Less Est. Usageᵇ	23,436	26,784	26,784	30,132	30,132	33,480	20,088	20,088	30,132	33,480	33,480	26,784	334,800	334,800
End. Inv. if No Pur.	22,564													(288,800)
Purchases													371,800ᶜ	371,800ᶜ
End. Inv.														83,000ᵈ

ᵃFrom latest available balance sheet.
ᵇFrom Exhibit 48, where it was determined on a % per month basis.
ᶜEnd. Inv.   83,000
  Beg. Inv. 46,000
  Increase   37,000
  Usage   334,800
  Purchases 371,800
ᵈCalculated at $83,000 on the basis of an 80% increase, or $900,000 of production vs. $500,000 of sales last year.

Exhibit 49

TIMING OF MATERIAL PURCHASES

	A PRODUCTION PERCENTAGE	B "ONE MONTH LEAD TIME"	C % FROM "B" APPLIED TO $371,800
January	7%	8%	$29,744
February	8	8	29,744
March	8	9	33,462
April	9	9	33,462
May	9	10	37,180
June	10	6	22,308
July	6	6	22,308
August	6	9	33,462
September	9	10	37,180
October	10	10	37,180
November	10	8[a]	29,744
December	8	7[b]	26,026
TOTAL	100%	100%	$371,800

[a]Subtotal of 93%.
[b]"Plug" of 7% to total 100%.

Exhibit 50

worth of sales dollar production was determined (see Exhibit 54). As shown on the Exhibit, it is estimated that total labor costs for this production effort would run $288,000.00. This type of information is based on the best data available, and how good this information is usually relates to the quality of the company's cost information. It may range from sophisticated cost accounting records to an educated guess.

Next, the question of *when* the labor would be expended arose. It will be recalled that we have already determined what an equal monthly effort would amount to, and also what the best guess is as to the productive effort curve. The estimated labor usage was next estimated, by production people, based on the production curve and other information. For example, although the productive effort would be less in July and August because of vacations, the actual amount of labor dollars used up during this period would not be that much less because vacation pay is involved. Vacation pay is also, therefore, a factor to be considered in determining unit labor costs.

The determination of labor usage is shown in Exhibit 55, which also shows for reference the "equal effort" distribution over the year and the production curve.

MANUFACTURING EXPENSES

Expenses are something that can be considered in detail, and notes should be made in a notebook as to the assumptions made for each item. Manufacturing expenses partake of a particular character: part of them (such as supplies for

RAW MATERIALS (THROUGH PURCHASES)

	JAN.	FEB.	MAR.	APR.	MAY	JUNE	JULY	AUG.	SEPT.	OCT.	NOV.	DEC.	TOTAL	"PROOF"
Beg. Inv.	46,000[a]													46,000[a]
Less Est. Usage[b]	23,436	26,784	26,784	30,132	30,132	33,480	20,088	20,088	30,132	33,480	33,480	26,784	334,800	334,800
End. Inv. if No Pur.	22,564													(288,800)
Purchases[c]	29,744	29,744	33,462	33,462	37,180	22,308	22,308	33,462	37,180	37,180	29,744	26,026	371,800[d]	371,800[e]
End. Inv.														83,000[e]

[a] From latest available balance sheet.
[b] From Exhibit 48, where it was determined on a % per month basis.
[c] From "Purchases" Schedule—See Exhibit 50.
[d]
End. Inv.	83,000
Beg. Inv.	46,000
Increase	37,000
Usage	334,800
Purchases	371,800
[e] Calculated at $83,000 on the basis of an 80% increase, or $900,000 of production vs. $500,000 of sales last year.

Exhibit 51

RAW MATERIALS (THROUGH ENDING INVENTORY)

	JAN.	FEB.	MAR.	APR.	MAY	JUNE	JULY	AUG.	SEPT.	OCT.	NOV.	DEC.	TOTAL	"PROOF"
Beg. Inv.	46,000[a]	52,308[b]	55,268	61,946	65,276	72,324	61,152	63,372	76,746	83,794	87,494	83,758		46,000[a]
Less Est. Usage[c]	23,436	26,784	26,784	30,132	30,132	33,480	20,088	20,088	30,132	33,480	33,480	26,784	334,800	334,800
End. Inv. if No Pur.	22,564	25,524	28,484	31,814	35,144	38,844	41,064	43,284	46,614	50,314	54,014	56,974		(288,800)
Purchases[d]	29,744	29,744	33,462	33,462	37,180	22,308	22,308	33,462	37,180	37,180	29,744	26,026	371,800[e]	371,800[e]
End. Inv.	52,308[f]	55,268	61,946	65,276	72,324	61,152	63,372	76,746	83,794	87,494	83,758	83,000	83,000[g]	83,000[g]

[a] From latest available balance sheet.
[b] Carried forward from end of previous month.
[c] From Exhibit 48, where it was determined on a % per month basis.
[d] From "Purchases" Schedule—See Exhibit 50.
[e]
End. Inv.	83,000
Beg. Inv.	46,000
Increase	37,000
Usage	334,800
Purchases	371,800
[f] 22,564 plus 29,744.
[g] Calculated at $83,000 on the basis of an 80% increase, or $900,000 of production vs. $500,000 of sales last year.

Exhibit 52

machines and those consumed in connection with the fabrication of a product) rise and fall with the tempo of manufacturing activity. On the other hand, there are elements (such as depreciation) that represent more or less *fixed* overhead. For the reason that the category of manufacturing expenses has this dual nature, it is especially helpful to predict manufacturing expenses, or to analyze past figures, in *detail*.

There are at least two approaches—the annual approach and the monthly approach—that can be taken in building up manufacturing expenses. In this instance, it was found most desirable to work up the figures on a monthly basis. As an example of the *type* of detailed reasoning utilized in the projection, here is how the various items shown in Exhibit 56 were calculated:

Supervisory salaries did include one man at $9,000 per year, and one man at $7,000. This year, with increases of $1,500 for the first man (who was almost hired away by a competitor) and $500 for the second man, there is an $18,000 budget figure instead of $16,000 with staff "as is." In fact, however, one man being paid $7,200 per year was just hired, and plans call for a second man, at $4,800 per year, to start in July. With $200.00 a month for raises, beginning in September, this completes the projection for this item.

Last year *indirect labor* consisted of one man at $5,500 a year, and two men at $4,000 each. This year's plans call for raises of $500 and $300 respectively, and the addition of one new man beginning "as soon as we can hire him" (so he is in the projection beginning in January) for approximately $6,000 per annum, plus one clerk at approximately $3,265 per year, beginning in August. A considerable amount of new production equipment is projected for this year, and looking at a rough outline of these additions, the office manager estimated that *depreciation* should be allowed at the rate of $800 a month for the first six months, and $1,200 a month thereafter.

The *repairs and maintenance* item contains some specific matters that will need attention in the first quarter, so this item was scheduled at $1,000 a month for the first three months, and the balance of the annual estimate spread more or less equally throughout the rest of the year.

It is estimated that *supplies,* which relate to machine and shop production efforts, will be expended (more or less) in keeping with the tempo which is planned for production: specifically, that, of the year's production, 7 percent, will take place in the months of January, February, March and April; that 8 percent will be used in May and June; 9 percent in July, August, September, and October; and 10 percent each in the months of November and December. Accordingly, the total year's estimate for usage of supplies was allocated in these proportions.

Payroll taxes, of course, run in proportion to the salaries and wages to which they relate, and these estimates have been prorated approximately in keeping with these payments.

Engineering expense relates specifically to some projects that will be carried out principally in the months of March and April, and therefore these known expenses have been shown for those months, with the balance of the item representing routine charges which tend to be repetitive. (Actually, the charges of this nature may eventually be capitalized, and more properly shown as an amortization over a longer period of time. But, at this juncture, management chose to view them as strictly expense.)

PROJECTED PROFIT AND LOSS STATEMENT

		JAN.	FEB.	MAR.	APR.	MAY
GROSS SALES		57,000	65,000	65,000	41,000	49,000
(Less: Returns & Allow.)		(570)	(650)	(650)	(410)	(490)
NET SALES		56,430	64,350	64,350	40,590	48,510
COST OF GOODS SOLD:						
Cost of Goods Mfg'd.:						
Beg. Inv., WIP		9,000	10,500	12,000	13,500	15,000
(Less End. Inv., WIP)		(10,500)	(12,000)	(13,500)	(15,000)	(16,500)
Change, WIP	*	(1,500)	(1,500)	(1,500)	(1,500)	(1,500)
Beg. Inv., Raw Mat'l.		46,000	52,308	55,268	61,946	65,276
Purchases		29,744	29,744	33,462	33,462	37,180
Goods Available		75,744	82,052	88,730	95,408	102,456
(Less End. Inv., R. M.)		(52,308)	(55,268)	(61,946)	(65,276)	(72,324)
Materials Used	*	23,436	26,784	26,784	30,132	30,132
Labor Used	*					
Manufacturing Expenses	*					
TOTAL, C. OF G. M.	*					
Cost of Goods Sold:						
Beg. Inv., Fin. Gds.						
Cost of Gds. Mfg'd.						
Goods Available						
(Less End. Inv., F. Gds.)						
TOTAL, C. OF G. S.						
GROSS PROFIT						
EXPENSES:						
Sales Expense						
Gen'l. & Admin. Expense						
TOTAL EXPENSES						
OPERATING PROFIT						
OTHER INCOME (OTHER CHARGES)—NET						
PROFIT BEFORE INCOME TAXES						
PROVISION FOR INCOME TAXES						
PROFIT AFTER INCOME TAXES						

Exhibit 53

The *miscellaneous* account is "just that," and an approximate figure, revised upward in keeping with general productive activity, was simply apportioned out more or less equally.

Adding up all of the above, we get the $91,000 budget which was built up from details. A *cost* system approach, however, yielded a higher figure—$97,200— and at this point the matter was resolved by *including* in the *manufacturing expenses* projection an item representing the difference of $6,200 between the two estimates.

(THROUGH MATERIALS USED)

JUNE	JULY	AUG.	SEPT.	OCT.	NOV.	DEC.	TOTAL
57,000	65,000	73,000	88,000	81,000	88,000	81,000	810,000
(570)	(650)	(730)	(880)	(810)	(880)	(810)	(8,100)
56,430	64,350	72,270	87,120	80,190	87,120	80,190	801,900
16,500	18,000	19,500	21,000	22,500	24,000	25,500	9,000
(18,000)	(19,500)	(21,000)	(22,500)	(24,000)	(25,500)	(27,000)	(27,000)
(1,500)	(1,500)	(1,500)	(1,500)	(1,500)	(1,500)	(1,500)	(18,000)
72,324	61,152	63,372	76,746	83,794	87,494	83,758	46,000
22,308	22,308	33,462	37,180	37,180	29,744	26,026	371,800
94,632	83,460	96,834	113,926	120,974	117,238	109,784	417,800
(61,152)	(63,372)	(76,746)	(83,794)	(87,494)	(83,758)	(83,000)	(83,000)
33,480	20,088	20,088	30,132	33,480	33,480	26,784	334,800

Exhibit 53 (cont'd)

In other words, to hold the broad, overall projection to conservative proportions, management decided—for the purpose of present projection purposes, at least—to "budget" for the extra $6,200. (But, you can be sure that if any of this is needed, there had better be awfully good explanations!)

Exhibit 56 shows how the company estimated in detail the manufacturing expenses for each month for the nine different items, with a total for the month and a total for the year. This type of data is most useful in the months ahead, as one

ESTIMATED LABOR COSTS

	A UNIT PRICE	B EST. UNIT LABOR COST	C LABOR AS % OF SALES PRICE (B DIV. A)	D EST. VOLUME OF PRODUCTION	EST. LABOR COSTS (C × D)
Product A	$500.00	$159.00	31.8%	$160,000	$ 50,880
B	200.00	62.40	31.2	85,000	26,520
C	500.00	146.00	29.2	155,000	45,260
D	600.00	201.60	33.6	320,000	107,520
E	300.00	96.60	32.2	160,000	51,520
Service	——	——	29.2[a]	15,000	4,380
Misc.	——	——	39.2[a]	5,000	1,920
		TOTAL		$900,000	$288,000

[a]Arbitrary estimate.

Exhibit 54

ESTIMATED LABOR USAGE

	"EQUAL"		"PRODUCTION"		ESTIMATED	
	MO.	CUM.	MO.	CUM.	LABOR %	USAGE $
January	8.33%	8.33%	7%	7%	7%	$ 20,160
February	"	16.66	8	15	7	20,160
March	"	24.99	8	23	8	23,040
April	"	33.32	9	32	8	23,040
May	"	41.65	9	41	8	23,040
June	"	49.98	10	51	8	23,040
July	"	58.31	6	57	8	23,040
August	"	66.64	6	63	9	25,920
September	"	74.97	9	72	9	25,920
October	"	83.30	10	82	9	25,920
November	"	91.63	10	92	9	25,920
December	"	99.99	8	100	10	28,800
	100.00%		100%		100%	$288,000

Exhibit 55

becomes able to compare actual performance with projected performance. But the information will be no more useful than the notes are detailed.

Next, the information on labor and manufacturing expenses can be transferred

MANUFACTURING EXPENSES—DETAILED

	JAN.	FEB.	MAR.	APR.	MAY	JUNE	JULY	AUG.	SEPT.	OCT.	NOV.	DEC.	TOTAL
Supervis. Salaries	2,100	2,100	2,100	2,100	2,100	2,100	2,500	2,500	2,600	2,600	2,600	2,600	28,000
Indirect Labor	1,720	1,720	1,720	1,720	1,720	1,720	1,720	1,992	1,992	1,992	1,992	1,992	22,000
Depreciation	800	800	800	800	800	800	1,200	1,200	1,200	1,200	1,200	1,200	12,000
Repairs & Mtce.	1,000	1,000	1,000	300	300	200	200	200	200	200	200	200	5,000
Supplies	700	700	700	700	800	800	900	900	900	900	1,000	1,000	10,000
Payroll Taxes	150	150	150	150	150	150	150	190	190	190	190	190	2,000
Engineering Exp.	500	500	2,500	2,500	500	500	500	500	500	500	500	500	10,000
Misc.	150	150	150	150	150	150	150	150	150	150	250	250	2,000
"Unallocated"	500	500	500	500	500	500	500	500	500	500	600	600	6,200
TOTAL	7,620	7,620	9,620	8,920	7,020	6,920	7,820	8,132	8,232	8,232	8,532	8,532	97,200

Exhibit 56

PROJECTED PROFIT AND LOSS STATEMENT

		JAN.	FEB.	MAR.	APR.	MAY
GROSS SALES		57,000	65,000	65,000	41,000	49,000
(Less: Returns & Allow.)		(570)	(650)	(650)	(410)	(490)
NET SALES		56,430	64,350	64,350	40,590	48,510
COST OF GOODS SOLD:						
Cost of Goods Mfg'd.:						
Beg. Inv., WIP		9,000	10,500	12,000	13,500	15,000
(Less End. Inv., WIP)		(10,500)	(12,000)	(13,500)	(15,000)	(16,500)
Change, WIP	*	(1,500)	(1,500)	(1,500)	(1,500)	(1,500)
Beg. Inv., Raw Mat'l.		46,000	52,308	55,268	61,946	65,276
Purchases		29,744	29,744	33,462	33,462	37,180
Goods Available		75,744	82,052	88,730	95,408	102,456
(Less End. Inv., R. M.)		(52,308)	(55,268)	(61,946)	(65,276)	(72,324)
Materials Used	*	23,436	26,784	26,784	30,132	30,132
Labor Used	*	20,160	20,160	23,040	23,040	30,132
Manufacturing Expenses	*	7,620	7,620	9,620	8,920	7,020
TOTAL, C. OF G. M.	*	49,716	53,064	57,944	60,592	58,692
Cost of Goods Sold:						
Beg. Inv., Fin. Gds.						
Cost of Gds. Mfg'd.		49,716	53,064	57,944	60,592	58,692
Goods Available						
(Less End. Inv., F. Gds.)						
TOTAL, C. OF G. S.						
GROSS PROFIT						
EXPENSES:						
Sales Expense						
Gen'l. & Admin. Expense						
TOTAL EXPENSES						
OPERATING PROFIT						
OTHER INCOME (OTHER CHARGES)—NET						
PROFIT BEFORE INCOME TAXES						
PROVISION FOR INCOME TAXES						
PROFIT AFTER INCOME TAXES						

Exhibit 57

to our evolving P. & L. statement. The way it will appear after this information is posted is shown in Exhibit 57.

Notice also, in Exhibit 57, that the cost of goods manufactured has been carried *down* to the next section of the P. & L. statement, which deals with finished goods. As this suggests, the next thing we must deal with is the latter.

(THROUGH COST OF GOODS MANUFACTURED)

JUNE	JULY	AUG.	SEPT.	OCT.	NOV.	DEC.	TOTAL
57,000	65,000	73,000	88,000	81,000	88,000	81,000	810,000
(570)	(650)	(730)	(880)	(810)	(880)	(810)	(8,100)
56,430	64,350	72,270	87,120	80,190	87,120	80,190	801,900
16,500	18,000	19,500	21,000	22,500	24,000	25,500	9,000
(18,000)	(19,500)	(21,000)	(22,500)	(24,000)	(25,500)	(27,000)	(27,000)
(1,500)	(1,500)	(1,500)	(1,500)	(1,500)	(1,500)	(1,500)	(18,000)
72,324	61,152	63,372	76,746	83,794	87,494	83,758	46,000
22,308	22,308	33,462	37,180	37,180	29,744	26,026	371,800
94,632	83,460	96,834	113,926	120,974	117,238	109,784	417,800
(61,152)	(63,372)	(76,746)	(83,794)	(87,494)	(83,758)	(83,000)	(83,000)
33,480	20,088	20,088	30,132	33,480	33,480	26,784	334,800
23,040	23,040	25,920	25,920	25,920	25,920	28,800	288,000
6,920	7,820	8,132	8,232	8,232	8,532	8,532	97,200
61,940	49,448	52,640	62,784	66,132	66,432	62,616	702,000
61,940	49,448	52,640	62,784	66,132	66,432	62,616	702,000

Exhibit 57 (cont'd)

FINISHED GOODS

Next, management had to determine what would be the ending inventory of finished goods, at the close of the year. After giving considerable attention to this matter, and weighing the various factors of production and the fact that the company was producing $900,000.00 worth of goods during the period, without expecting that sales would equal this amount, an ending inventory figure of $122,100.00 was determined. This may sound like an odd amount, but it really resulted from approaching the subject both from a totals viewpoint and also from the viewpoint of a specific number of units with a specific cost to be carried at the end of the year. In any event, as shown on Exhibit 58, by using the formula that is basic for cost of goods sold, the company management arrived at a cost of goods sold figure for the year. Next, this was related to the gross sales figure and the cost of sales was reduced to a percentage, which turned out to be 77.77 percent.

COST OF GOODS SOLD CALCULATION

Beginning Inventory, Fin. Gds.	$ 50,000	
Cost of Goods Manufactured	702,000	
Available	$752,000	
(Less: End. Inv., Fin. Goods)	122,100	(Arbitrarily determined)
Cost of Goods Sold	$629,900	
Gross Sales	$810,000	100.00%
(Returns & Allow.)	(8,100)	(1.00)
Net Sales	$801,900	99.00
Cost of Goods Sold	$629,900	77.77%

Exhibit 58

MONTHLY COST OF GOODS SOLD

	GROSS SALES	× 77.77% EQUALS C. OF G. S.
January	$ 57,000	$ 44,329
February	65,000	50,551
March	65,000	50,551
April	41,000	31,886
May	49,000	38,107
June	57,000	44,329
July	65,000	50,551
August	73,000	56,772
September	88,000	68,438
October	81,000	62,994
November	88,000	68,438
December	81,000	62,954[a]
	$810,000	$629,900

[a]Adjusted so total is $629,900.

Exhibit 59

FINISHED GOODS INVENTORY (THROUGH COST OF GOODS SOLD)

	JAN.	FEB.	MAR.	APR.	MAY	JUNE	JULY	AUG.	SEPT.	OCT.	NOV.	DEC.	TOTAL
Beg. Inv., Fin. Gds.	50,000[a]												50,000[a]
Cost of Gds. Mf'd.[b]	49,716	53,064	57,944	60,592	58,692	61,940	49,448	52,640	62,784	66,132	66,432	62,616	702,000
Goods Available													
(Less: C. of Gds. Sold)[c]	(44,329)	(50,551)	(50,551)	(31,886)	(38,107)	(44,329)	(50,551)	(56,772)	(68,438)	(62,994)	(68,438)	(62,954)	(629,900)
Fin. Gds. Inv.													

[a]Known from latest balance sheet.
[b]From Exhibit 57.
[c]From Exhibit 59.

Exhibit 60

FINISHED GOODS INVENTORY—COMPLETE

	JAN.	FEB.	MAR.	APR.	MAY	JUNE	JULY	AUG.	SEPT.	OCT.	NOV.	DEC.	TOTAL
Beg. Inv., Fin. Gds.	50,000[a]	55,387	57,900	65,293	93,999	114,584	132,195	131,092	126,960	121,306	124,444	122,438	50,000
Cost of Gds. Mf'd.[b]	49,716	53,064	57,944	60,592	58,692	61,940	49,448	52,640	62,784	66,132	66,432	62,616	702,000
Gds. Available[c]	99,716	108,451	115,844	125,885	152,691	176,524	181,643	183,732	189,744	187,438	190,876	185,054	752,000
(Less: C. of Gds. Sold)[d]	(44,329)	(50,551)	(50,551)	(31,886)	(38,107)	(44,329)	(50,551)	(56,772)	(68,438)	(62,994)	(68,438)	(62,954)	(629,900)
Fin. Gds. Inv.[e]	55,387	57,900	65,293	93,999	114,584	132,195	131,092	126,960	121,306	124,444	122,438	122,100	122,100

[a]Known from latest balance sheet.
[b]From Exhibit 57.
[c]Subtotal, Beg. Inv. plus C. of Gds. Mfg'd.
[d]From Exhibit 59.
[e]Gds. Available, less C. of Gds. Sold, carried forward to next month.

Exhibit 61

PROJECTED PROFIT AND LOSS STATEMENT

		JAN.	FEB.	MAR.	APR.	MAY
GROSS SALES		57,000	65,000	65,000	41,000	49,000
(Less: Returns & Allow.)		(570)	(650)	(650)	(410)	(490)
NET SALES		56,430	64,350	64,350	40,590	48,510
COST OF GOODS SOLD:						
Cost of Goods Mfg'd.:						
Beg. Inv., WIP		9,000	10,500	12,000	13,500	15,000
(Less End. Inv., WIP)		(10,500)	(12,000)	(13,500)	(15,000)	(16,500)
Change, WIP	*	(1,500)	(1,500)	(1,500)	(1,500)	(1,500)
Beg. Inv., Raw Mat'l.		46,000	52,308	55,268	61,946	65,276
Purchases		29,744	29,744	33,462	33,462	37,180
Goods Available		75,744	82,052	88,730	95,408	102,456
(Less End. Inv., R. M.)		(52,308)	(55,268)	(61,946)	(65,276)	(72,324)
Materials Used	*	23,436	26,784	26,784	30,132	30,132
Labor Used	*	20,160	20,160	23,040	23,040	23,040
Manufacturing Expenses	*	7,620	7,620	9,620	8,920	7,020
TOTAL, C. OF G. M.	*	49,716	53,064	57,944	60,592	58,692
Cost of Goods Sold:						
Beg. Inv., Fin. Gds.		50,000	55,387	57,900	65,293	93,999
Cost of Gds. Mf'd.		49,716	53,064	57,944	60,592	58,692
Goods Available		99,716	108,451	115,844	125,885	152,691
(Less End. Inv. F. Gds.)		(55,387)	(57,900)	(65,293)	(93,999)	(114,584)
TOTAL, C. OF G. S.		44,329	50,551	50,551	31,886	38,107
GROSS PROFIT		12,101	13,799	13,799	8,704	10,403
EXPENSES:						
Sales Expense						
Gen'l. & Admin. Expense						
TOTAL EXPENSE						
OPERATING PROFIT						
OTHER INCOME (OTHER CHARGES)—NET						
PROFIT BEFORE INCOME TAXES						
PROVISION FOR INCOME TAXES						
PROFIT AFTER INCOME TAXES						

Exhibit 62

GROSS PROFIT

Having determined the percentage of cost of goods sold, and knowing what the estimated sales are going to be for each month, all that was necessary next, in order to come up with a monthly cost of goods sold figure, was to multiply 77.77 percent times the gross sales for each month, as has been done in Exhibit 59.

Next, a work sheet was prepared as shown in Exhibit 60, giving effect to the

(THROUGH COST OF GOODS SOLD)

JUNE	JULY	AUG.	SEPT.	OCT.	NOV.	DEC.	TOTAL
57,000	65,000	73,000	88,000	81,000	88,000	81,000	810,000
(570)	(650)	(730)	(880)	(810)	(880)	(810)	(8,100)
56,430	64,350	72,270	87,120	80,190	87,120	80,190	801,900
16,500	18,000	19,500	21,000	22,500	24,000	25,500	9,000
(18,000)	(19,500)	(21,000)	(22,500)	(24,000)	(25,500)	(27,000)	(27,000)
(1,500)	(1,500)	(1,500)	(1,500)	(1,500)	(1,500)	(1,500)	(18,000)
72,324	61,152	63,372	76,746	83,794	87,494	83,758	46,000
22,308	22,308	33,462	37,180	37,180	29,744	26,026	371,800
94,632	83,460	96,834	113,926	120,974	117,238	109,784	417,800
(61,152)	(63,372)	(76,746)	(83,794)	(87,494)	(83,758)	(83,000)	83,000
33,480	20,088	20,088	30,132	33,480	33,480	26,784	334,800
23,040	23,040	25,920	25,920	25,920	25,920	28,800	288,000
6,920	7,820	8,132	8,232	8,232	8,532	8,532	97,200
61,940	49,448	52,640	62,784	66,132	66,432	62,616	702,000
114,584	132,195	131,092	126,960	121,306	124,444	122,438	50,000
61,940	49,448	52,640	62,784	66,132	66,432	62,616	702,000
176,524	181,643	183,732	189,744	187,438	190,876	185,054	752,000
(132,195)	(131,092)	(126,960)	(121,306)	(124,444)	(122,438)	(122,100)	(122,100)
44,329	50,551	56,772	68,438	62,994	68,438	62,954	629,900
12,101	13,799	15,498	18,682	17,196	18,682	17,236	172,000

Exhibit 62 (cont'd)

information that we have, which is the cost of goods manufactured for each month, as determined previously, the beginning inventory of finished goods, and the monthly cost of goods sold. This last item, of course, represents what is moving out of inventory each month. All that is necessary, then, is to complete the work sheet, as shown in Exhibit 61.

This work sheet (Exhibit 61) gives us the information we need to complete the finished goods section of the P. & L. statement. Once we have the cost of goods sold, which this gives us, we are also able to go ahead and determine the gross profit, by subtracting the cost of goods sold from the gross sales figure. Exhibit 62 shows the P. & L. statement as it will appear with all the information down to gross profit posted to it.

FOR TRADING COMPANIES

As suggested earlier, the determination of *cost of sales* and all of the related factors for a wholesaler or retailer is relatively easy, as compared to that for a manufacturer.

For a trading company the *key fact* you need to establish is *gross profit percentage*. Once you "know" that, you can apply the percentage to your sales figure and get (1) *dollar* gross profits and (2) by interpolation, dollar *cost of sales*. The basic formula you must deal with is still the same:

1.	Beginning Inventory	300
2.	*Plus* Purchases	150
3.	gives "Subtotal" (or "Available for Sale")	450
4.	*less* Cost of Sales	(125)
5.	gives Ending Inventory	325

And as is so often the case in projecting, you move "from the *known* to the unknown." Usually you will *know* (1) the first month's beginning inventory and (2) the dollar cost of sales (determined by applying 100 percent less the gross profit percentage factor to sales). You will want to *find out* (3) the purchases for each period and (4) the ending inventory for each period (which, of course, also supplies the beginning inventory figures for the periods *after* the first one).

Next we come to the generally recognized method of *relating* cost of sales to inventory: "Days' Cost of Sales in Inventory." Say, for the sake of illustration, that the management considers a *60*-day supply of inventory adequate for the period ahead. Next you *divide* the dollar *cost of sales* figures for each period by *30*, to get what *one* days' cost of sales amounts to, then you multiply the result by *60*—which gives you the *desired* ending inventory figures. With them, you set up a schedule to do, once again, some "formula twisting," and you determine the elusive *purchases* figure:

1.	Beginning Inventory (known)	300
2.	*Less* Cost of Sales (known)	(125)
3.	Ending Inventory if there are no purchases (1 – 2)	175
4.	*Desired* Ending Inventory (known)	325
5.	Purchases Necessary to obtain desired Ending Inventory (4 – 3)	150

In some cases management will want to depart from this format to some extent, using *known purchases* data, and *find out* what the resulting inventory position would be—in which case the formula would be:

1. Beginning Inventory   300
2. Plus Purchases   150
3. Gives "To Be Accounted For"   450
4. Less "Cost of Sales" (what will *move
    out* of Inventory)   (125)
5. Gives Resulting Inventory (3 − 4)   325

Another sometimes useful twist: to say, in planning, "at the *end* of January I want a *two month* supply (or what have you) on hand in inventory." Then, to get at what that *means,* as an ending inventory figure, you just look back at your schedule of what cost of sales is for the two months *ahead* (February and March), and use *that* figure for the January ending inventory—etc.

WHAT NEXT?

Now there remains the job of completing the P. & L. statement, and this task is treated in the next chapter.

11

Completion of the P. & L.

It is difficult to exaggerate the opportunities for reduced marketing costs and increased marketing efficiency, and hence greater profits, which are offered to management by the combined techniques of distribution cost analysis and mathematical programing. In the offing may be a revolution in the planning and execution of distribution that is fully comparable to the triumph of time and motion studies and cost analysis in the factory. . . . The separation of (a) fixed costs incurred in common for different types of sales effort, (b) separable fixed costs and (c) variable costs which are related to different segments of the business is one of the key steps in analyzing a company's distribution problem.

—Page 247, *New Decision-Making Tools for Managers,*
Mentor Executive Library Book, May, 1965

GENERAL APPROACH

BY NOW YOU KNOW WHAT TO EXPECT: DETAILED ESTIMATES starting with the *smallest* category, on a *monthly* basis, for a year ahead. As always, with one eye on the past and the other on the *future,* an attempt is made to make the numerous *individual* estimates on the most *realistic* basis possible. And, please remember, it is *most* important to "preserve your thinking," item by item, so that a year from now (and more likely *each month* during the coming year) you can refer back to your notes and draw meaningful conclusions as you compare your forecast with *actual* figures.

The foregoing process has been demonstrated in previous chapters; here, to speed along our projection process, we will *not* record (as you actually would, in practice) all of the detailed thinking behind the estimates for each individual item of expense. Just pretend that you have gone through this process on each item. In a few instances the reasoning used will be explained.

With reference to the quotation at the beginning of this chapter, there is an *additional* reason to record the detailed data: without these "clues" as to the real *function* of the expenses, a manager is not *able* to take advantage of the latest type of analytical techniques (distribution cost analysis and mathematical programing, for example) to reduce costs and maximize the results of expenses.

SALES EXPENSES

Every dollar forecast was considered separately. For example, the advertising figures were determined only after *first* preparing a careful month-by-month outline of advertising *activity* contemplated in the year ahead. Then a price tag was applied to the entire program, the separate totals added up, and the "first draft" of the forecast was obtained. Next the whole picture was reviewed with particular reference to the expenses incurred *last* year; adjustments were made, and then (and *only* then) were the final projection figures entered in the proper section of the profit and loss statement (see Exhibit 63.)

It is interesting to note the following relationships that evolved from the projection process:

	LAST YEAR	YEAR AHEAD	$ INCREASE	% CHANGE
Gross Sales	$500,000	$810,000	$310,000	62%+
Sales Expenses	$31,000	$49,000	$18,000	58%+
Sales Expenses as a % of Gr. Sales	6.2%	6.0%	——	0.2%—

GENERAL AND ADMINISTRATIVE EXPENSES

Again the same process is followed; there is a "file" behind each item of G. & A. expenses. For example, note the increase in August and September in the item "Executive Salaries" (see Exhibit 64). This reflects the fact that at this time management plans to make an officer out of a new man to be added to the organization at an annual salary of $12,000 and that at the same time the president of the company would get a raise of $4,800 a year (only $200 of which is scheduled for the month of August).

When the item "Interest" was considered, management was confronted with a sort of "chicken or egg" dilemma: there was a *need* to know what interest would run, so the P. & L. projection could be completed, but at the same time it is *impossible* to "know" what *borrowings* will be required (and, of course, the amount of interest

PROJECTED SALES EXPENSES—DETAILED

	JAN.	FEB.	MAR.	APR.	MAY	JUNE	JULY	AUG.	SEPT.	OCT.	NOV.	DEC.	TOTAL
Salaries & Comm.	1,800	1,900	2,000	2,200	2,400	2,500	2,600	2,700	2,800	3,000	3,000	3,100	30,000
Travel & Enter.	300	300	400	400	400	400	500	600	600	700	700	700	6,000
Advertising	500	600	600	700	700	800	800	800	800	900	900	900	9,000
Delivery Exp.	150	150	200	200	200	250	250	300	300	300	350	350	3,000
Depreciation	50	50	50	50	50	50	100	100	100	100	150	150	1,000
TOTAL	2,800	3,000	3,250	3,550	3,750	4,000	4,250	4,500	4,600	5,000	5,100	5,200	49,000

Exhibit 63

GENERAL ADMINISTRATIVE EXPENSES—DETAILED

	JAN.	FEB.	MAR.	APR.	MAY	JUNE	JULY	AUG.	SEPT.	OCT.	NOV.	DEC.	TOTAL
Executive Salaries	1,600	1,600	1,600	1,600	1,600	1,600	1,600	2,800	3,000	3,000	3,000	3,000	26,000
Office Salaries	900	900	900	1,200	1,200	1,200	1,200	1,300	1,300	1,300	1,300	1,300	14,000
Office Supplies & Stationery	50	50	50	50	100	100	100	100	100	100	100	100	1,000
Postage	50	50	50	50	50	50	50	50	50	50	50	50	600
Telephone	100	100	100	100	100	100	100	100	100	100	200	200	1,400
Professional Services	125	125	125	125	125	125	125	125	125	125	125	125	1,500
Insurance—General	200	200	200	200	200	200	200	200	200	200	200	300	2,500
Insurance—Emp. Hospitaliz.	100	100	100	100	100	100	100	100	100	100	200	200	1,400
Payroll Taxes	100	100	100	100	200	200	200	200	200	200	200	200	2,000
Personal Property Taxes	50	50	50	50	50	50	50	50	50	50	100	100	700
Real Estate Taxes	100	100	100	100	100	100	100	100	100	200	200	200	1,500
Bad Debts	200	200	200	200	200	200	200	200	200	400	400	400	3,000
Collection Expense	—	—	50	50	50	50	50	50	50	50	50	50	500
Dues & Subscriptions	25	25	25	25	25	25	25	25	25	25	25	25	300
Bank Charges	30	30	30	30	30	30	30	30	40	40	40	40	400
Depreciation	15	15	15	15	15	15	15	15	15	15	25	25	200
Interest	1,500	1,500	1,500	1,500	1,500	1,500	1,500	1,500	1,500	1,500	1,500	1,500	18,000
Utilities	50	50	50	50	100	100	100	100	100	100	100	100	1,000
Repairs & Maintenance	25	25	25	25	50	50	50	50	50	50	50	50	500
Misc.	25	25	25	25	25	25	25	25	25	25	25	25	300
TOTAL	5,245	5,245	5,295	5,595	5,820	5,820	5,820	7,120	7,330	7,630	7,890	7,990	76,800

Exhibit 64

PROJECTED PROFIT AND LOSS

		JAN.	FEB.	MAR.	APR.	MAY
GROSS SALES		57,000	65,000	65,000	41,000	49,000
(Less: Returns & Allow.)		(570)	(650)	(650)	(410)	(490)
NET SALES		56,430	64,350	64,350	40,590	48,510
COST OF GOODS SOLD:						
Cost of Goods Mfg'd.:						
Beg. Inv., WIP		9,000	10,500	12,000	13,500	15,000
(Less End. Inv., WIP)		(10,500)	(12,000)	(13,500)	(15,000)	(16,500)
Change, WIP	*	(1,500)	(1,500)	(1,500)	(1,500)	(1,500)
Beg. Inv., Raw Mat'l.		46,000	52,308	55,268	61,946	65,276
Purchases		29,744	29,744	33,462	33,462	37,180
Goods Available		75,744	82,052	88,730	95,408	102,456
(Less End. Inv., R. M.)		(52,308)	(55,268)	(61,946)	(65,276)	(72,324)
Materials Used	*	23,436	26,784	26,784	30,132	30,132
Labor Used	*	20,160	20,160	23,040	23,040	23,040
Manufacturing Expenses	*	7,620	7,620	9,620	8,920	7,020
TOTAL, C. OF G. M.	*	49,716	53,064	57,944	60,592	58,692
Cost of Goods Sold:						
Beg. Inv., Fin. Gds.		50,000	55,387	57,900	65,293	93,999
Cost of Gds. Mfg'd.		49,716	53,064	57,944	60,592	58,692
Goods Available		99,716	108,451	115,844	125,885	152,691
(Less End. Inv., F. Gds.)		(55,387)	(57,900)	(65,293)	(93,999)	(114,584)
TOTAL, C. OF G. S.		44,329	50,551	50,551	31,886	38,107
GROSS PROFIT		12,101	13,799	13,799	8,704	10,403
EXPENSES:						
Sales Expense		2,800	3,000	3,250	3,550	3,750
Gen'l. & Admin. Expense		5,245	5,245	5,295	5,595	5,820
TOTAL EXPENSES		8,045	8,245	8,545	9,145	9,570
OPERATING PROFIT		4,056	5,554	5,254	(441)	833
OTHER INCOME (OTHER CHARGES)—NET		(250)	(250)	(250)	(250)	(250)
PROFIT BEFORE INCOME TAXES		3,806	5,304	5,004	(691)	583
PROVISION FOR INCOME TAXES		952	1,326	1,251	(173)	146
PROFIT AFTER INCOME TAXES		2,854	3,978	3,753	(518)	437

Exhibit 65

STATEMENT—COMPLETED

JUNE	JULY	AUG.	SEPT.	OCT.	NOV.	DEC.	TOTAL
57,000	65,000	73,000	88,000	81,000	88,000	81,000	810,000
(570)	(650)	(730)	(880)	(810)	(880)	(810)	(8,100)
56,430	64,350	72,270	87,120	80,190	87,120	80,190	801,900
16,500	18,000	19,500	21,000	22,500	24,000	25,500	9,000
(18,000)	(19,500)	(21,000)	(22,500)	(24,000)	(25,500)	(27,000)	(27,000)
(1,500)	(1,500)	(1,500)	(1,500)	(1,500)	(1,500)	(1,500)	(18,000)
72,324	61,152	63,372	76,746	83,794	87,494	83,758	46,000
22,308	22,308	33,462	37,180	37,180	29,744	26,026	371,800
94,632	83,460	96,834	113,926	120,974	117,238	109,784	417,800
(61,152)	(63,372)	(76,746)	(83,794)	(87,494)	(83,758)	(83,000)	83,000
33,480	20,088	20,088	30,132	33,480	33,480	26,784	334,800
23,040	23,040	25,920	25,920	25,920	25,920	28,800	288,000
6,920	7,820	8,132	8,232	8,232	8,532	8,532	97,200
61,940	49,448	52,640	62,784	66,132	66,432	62,616	702,000
114,584	132,195	131,092	126,960	121,306	124,444	122,438	50,000
61,940	49,448	52,640	62,784	66,132	66,432	62,616	702,000
176,524	181,643	183,732	189,744	187,438	190,876	185,054	752,000
(132,195)	(131,092)	(126,960)	(121,306)	(124,444)	(122,438)	(122,100)	(122,100)
44,329	50,551	56,772	68,438	62,994	68,438	62,954	629,900
12,101	13,799	15,498	18,682	17,196	18,682	17,236	172,000
4,000	4,250	4,500	4,600	5,000	5,100	5,200	49,000
5,820	5,820	7,120	7,330	7,630	7,890	7,990	76,800
9,820	10,070	11,620	11,930	12,630	12,990	13,190	125,800
2,281	3,729	3,878	6,752	4,566	5,692	4,046	46,200
(250)	(250)	(250)	(250)	(250)	(250)	(250)	(3,000)
2,031	3,479	3,628	6,502	4,316	5,442	3,796	43,200
507	870	907	2,787	2,158	2,721	1,898	15,350
1,524	2,609	2,721	3,715	2,158	2,721	1,898	27,850

Exhibit 65 (cont'd)

costs to be incurred will be directly related to borrowings). This problem was met by approaching the calculation on the following basis:

	Interest
1. That *short-term bank* debt would average $88,000, as it was at last year's end, at 8 percent.	$7,040
2. The item "Current Maturities—$19,300" at last year's end breaks down as follows:	
a. Principal, R. E. Mtge., $5,000	
b. Interest at 7 percent, R. E. Mtge., $3,045 (average balance of $43,500 in year ahead)	3,045
c. Installment payments (principal *and* interest) on equipment notes and contracts—$11,255 with *interest* portion approximating $3,255	3,255
3. What interest *will* be *if* there is no more *new* debt	$13,340
4. Assuming *additional* short-term loans averaging $60,000 at 8 percent will be needed (at this *point,* simply an "educated guess"—*precise* estimates can be prepared later, when needs are better known)	4,800
	$18,140
	(Rounded to $18,000)

The "educated guess," incidentally, wasn't altogether just a "blind stab." Sales (as noted earlier) are forecast to increase 62 percent. A 62 percent increase in short-term borrowings would amount to $54,560, which was "rounded upward" to $60,000.

OTHER INCOME (OTHER CHARGES)

Actually, the nature of these items in this particular company is such that they are rather unpredictable. After a discussion management agreed that $3,000 would be shown as "Other Charges," even though no one could think of a particular expense for this category that would, for sure, be incurred. The amount was simply spread throughout the year (see Exhibit 65).

It is worth noting that some accountants regularly place in the other income category discounts earned, presumably on the premise that these are *not* "operating items" and that they deserve special attention, which of course they receive in this area. In this case, however, in order to be consistant with past practice the company shows discounts earned as a separate item later combined with purchases of materials; in being separate, attention is still focused on the item, and related percentages are available, but the item is treated as a regular operating factor. Similarly, some accountants like to show discounts allowed others here, while other accountants follow the practice used by this company, which is to include such items as a *deduction* from sales, under the general heading, "Returns and Allowances."

This type of item highlights why it is especially helpful for management to make careful notes of its assumptions, *while* the assumptions are being made. In this case, no one is particularly accountable for the items, and $3,000 is not an insignificant amount of money. Therefore, when something comes up on this item during the year, it is well for management to be able to review its *original* thinking with reference to the amounts.

INCOME TAXES

After sales expenses and general and administrative expenses were posted to the P. & L. (Exhibit 65), next it was possible (just by adding and subtracting) to fill in the lines "Total Expenses" and "Operating Profit" thereon. Then, after posting the "Other Income (Other Charges)—Net" figure to the P. & L., the simple process of subtraction will yield the figures to go on the line "Profit Before Income Taxes."

Federal income tax rates and regulations have changed somewhat over the years, and of course rates and regulations on *state* income taxes vary from state to

PROFITS, TAXES

	CUMULATIVE PROFIT BEFORE TAXES	CUMULATIVE TAX PROVISION
January	$ 3,806	$ 952[a]
February	5,304	1,326
	9,110	2,278
March	5,004	1,251
	14,114	3,529
April	(691)	(173)
	13,423	3,356
May	583	146
	14,006	3,502
June	2,031	507
	16,037	4,009
July	3,479	870
	19,516	4,879
August	3,628	907
	23,144	5,786
September	6,502	2,787[b]
	29,646	8,573
October	4,316	2,158[c]
	33,962	10,731
November	5,442	2,721
	39,404	13,452
December	3,796	1,898
	$43,200	$15,350

[a] At 25%, through August.
[b] At 25% on $25,000, 50% on $4,646.
[c] At 50% for balance of the year.

Exhibit 66

state. In this illustration it was assumed that a combined rate of 25 percent applies to up to $25,000 of profit, and a 50 percent rate applies to all profit over $25,000. On this basis the *cumulative* pretax profit and provision for income taxes figures were determined as shown in Exhibit 66.

The monthly provision figures were posted to the P. & L. (see Exhibit 65), and then, by subtraction, the last item on the P. & L., "Profit After Income Taxes," was determined.

"CROSSFOOTING"

Now that the P. & L. is complete, a suggestion: to make sure it "adds up" correctly and has "internal integrity," add all of the monthly columns *down* and then add the items *across,* finally adding the total column down. If all the figures "crossfoot" (agree), you know you won't be carrying forward some errors—which would arise to plague you later in the projection process.

12
Cash Flow

From time to time, we come across clients who do not actually realize where they are going, cashwise. In many cases, we will spend quite a bit of time with them. You might say that is something management should do itself. It certainly is. But many small businesses just do not have the time to devote to a detailed analysis of this sort. Many times we find that clients do not have too much cash to spare and are not too willing to pay their accountants to come in and spend a great deal more time on some of these things, vital as they may be. So that, by default, it is left to us, because we are looking to make it a healthy small business that we are financing, for our own protection as well as our client's.

> —MR. ROBERT A. KLEIN,
> President of National Business Credit Corporation,
> Newark, N. J. (a commercial finance company),
> 5/18/64, at a seminar held by the
> National Commercial Finance-Conference, Inc.
> (the trade association for commercial finance companies).

GENERAL APPROACH

EVEN TODAY, SOME RATHER SIMPLE BUSINESSES, AND EVEN CERtain types of very large businesses (for tax purposes—e.g., contractors), use a "cash" basis for their accounting. But generally speaking, a business must and/or should use the more widely accepted "accrual" basis of accounting, which simply means that income, costs, and expenses are accounted for on the basis of when they are *incurred,* instead of just when the cash may change hands.

The two accounts that represent the most significant effect of accrual basis accounting are *accounts receivable* and *accounts payable.* Receivables are important, since they represent money due you which will not be paid until sometime in the future—which ties up some of what would otherwise be your operating capital. It is not unusual for a company to do practically all of its business on a credit basis, and to have as much as a month's or two months' sales tied up or invested in its accounts receivable. On the other hand, payables represent the exercise of *your* credit ability, and in one sense the more creditors' funds you can use, the better, since the costs—if any—for such funds are relatively cheap. (Or, in some circumstances, using credit excessively may be quite expensive, when for example, you thereby lose a discount of 2 to 5 percent.) Thus the assumptions you make regarding how your cash flows *in* (through receivables) and *out* (mostly through payables) are most important: together they will in large measure determine how much money you will need to *borrow,* one of the principal reasons for using this projection process.

In deciding how to "guess" or forecast cash flow, once again we will use a detailed approach, taking each "small" factor, one at a time—hoping that in this manner we will, when we later put all of the individual estimates *together,* wind up with a more accurate and realistic overall projection. Remember this: the figures are, when totaled up and woven together properly, "going to tell *us*" what our cash needs are going to be; we assume, at this point in the projection process, that there are *no* limits to the funds that can be made available. We want the "diagnosis," whatever it is—*later,* well-armed with facts, figures, and an intricate but organized body of logic, we will worry about the problems. . . .

The process begins with the P. & L. statement, then goes on to the balance sheet —each report being used as a *checklist.* That is, each item on these statements is *considered* from a cash flow aspect: *is* there a cash flow effect, and if so, "what?," "when?," etc.

Turning first to the P. & L., we encounter "Sales"—and the cash flow of *this* activity is, of course, reflected in *accounts receivable,* so first we turn to the matter of estimating the collection of the accounts receivable, generated by sales.

COLLECTION OF RECEIVABLES

You will recall that earlier, when we were looking over the *past,* we discussed receivables, and that we discovered that the customary means of measuring their *amount,* in *relation* to *sales, is* to calculate "days' sales in accounts receivable." (Remember?—the balance of accounts receivable divided by sales, the result of this times 30 or 360 days, depending on whether you are figuring on a monthly or yearly basis.)

Examining the past (see Exhibit 6, p. 23), management decided after some discussion to use *57* days' sales as the basis for its estimate. We *have* a monthly *sales* figure, on our P. & L.; from it we determine what *one* day's sales amount to—then compute the balance at the end of the month on the basis of *57* days' sales being in the balance, and "presto"—we *have* our end-of-month receivables balance for each month during the projection process. (See Exhibit 67 for the calculations.)

CALCULATION OF END-OF-MONTH BALANCES—ACCOUNTS RECEIVABLE

	I NET SALES[a]	II ONE DAY'S SALES (COL. I. DIV. 30)	III 57 DAYS' (57 × COL. II.)[b]
January	$56,430	$1,881	$107,217
February	64,350	2,145	122,265
March	64,350	2,145	122,265
April	40,590	1,353	77,121
May	48,510	1,617	92,169
June	56,430	1,881	107,217
July	64,350	2,145	122,265
August	72,270	2,409	137,313
September	87,120	2,904	165,528
October	80,190	2,673	152,361
November	87,120	2,904	165,528
December	80,190	2,673	152,361

[a]From P. & L., Exhibit 65.
[b]Management decided to forecast on the basis of 57 days' sales in accounts receivable, so by multiplying 57 times Column II figures, the result in Column III, representing the estimated End-of-Month Balances for accounts receivable, was obtained.

Exhibit 67

Once again, using the now-familiar "proceed from the *known* to the *unknown*" principle, we move from the *now* known (above) end-of-month accounts receivables *balance* to get at what we *really* want to know, at this particular juncture: the *collections* (the cash flow inward) we can expect from the receivables. We make this next move by—once again—doing a little "formula-twisting." The basic applicable formula is:

1.	Beginning Balance, Receivables	100
	plus	
2.	Sales	70
3.	gives a "subtotal"	170
	minus	
4.	Collections	(50)
	yields	
5.	Ending Balance, Receivables	120

Now, we *know* (1) (from our last balance sheet), and we also *know* (2) (from our P. & L.) We do not know (4), but we *do* know (5). So—we use the *revised* formula:

CALCULATION OF MONTHLY COLLECTIONS—ACCOUNTS RECEIVABLE

	JAN.	FEB.	MAR.	APR.	MAY	JUNE	JULY	AUG.	SEPT.	OCT.	NOV.	DEC.	TOTAL ("PROOF")
1. Bal., Beg. of Mo.	78,000[a]												78,000[a]
2. Plus Net Sales[b]	56,430	64,350	64,350	40,590	48,510	56,430	64,350	72,270	87,120	80,190	87,120	80,190	801,900[b]
3. Equals "Subtotal"													
4. Less Balance, End of Mo.[c]	107,217	122,265	122,265	77,121	92,169	107,217	122,265	137,313	165,528	152,361	165,528	152,361	152,361[d]
5. Equals "Collections"	107,217	122,265	122,265	77,121	92,169	107,217	122,265	137,313	165,528	152,361	165,528	152,361	

[a]From 12-31 balance sheet (end of last year), Exhibit 31.

[b]From P. & L., Exhibit 65.

[c]From Exhibit 67.

[d]December balance, representing balance as of end of the projection year, entered here as it is needed to prove out the monthly calculations on an annual basis.

Exhibit 68

CALCULATION OF MONTHLY COLLECTIONS—ACCOUNTS RECEIVABLE—COMPLETE

	JAN.	FEB.	MAR.	APR.	MAY	JUNE	JULY	AUG.	SEPT.	OCT.	NOV.	DEC.	TOTAL ("PROOF")
1. Bal, Beg. of Mo.	78,000[a]	107,217[b]	122,265	122,265	77,121	92,169	107,217	122,265	137,313	165,528	152,361	165,528	78,000[a]
2. Plus Net Sales[c]	56,430	64,350	64,350	40,590	48,510	56,430	64,350	72,270	87,120	80,190	87,120	80,190	801,900[c]
3. Equals "Subtotal"[d]	134,430	171,567	186,615	162,855	125,631	148,599	171,567	194,535	224,433	245,718	239,481	245,718	879,900
4. Less Balance, End of Mo.[e]	107,217	122,265	122,265	77,121	92,169	107,217	122,265	137,313	165,528	152,361	165,528	152,361	152,361[f]
5. Equals "Collections"[g]	27,213	49,302	64,350	85,734	33,462	41,382	49,302	57,222	58,905	93,357	73,953	93,357	727,539[h]

[a]From 12-31 balance sheet (end of last year), Exhibit 31.
[b]The figure on line 4, in the Jan. column, is carried forward to line 1 in the Feb. column, etc. (that is, January's *ending* balance is February's *beginning* balance, etc.).
[c]From P. & L., Exhibit 65.
[d]Determined by *adding* figures on line 1 to figures on line 2.
[e]From Exhibit 67.
[f]December balance, representing balance as of end of the projection year, entered here as it is needed to prove out the monthly calculations on an annual basis.
[g]Obtained by *subtracting* figures on line 4 from figures on line 3.
[h]To "prove" this entire calculation, you must obtain this figure *both* by (1) adding "across" the twelve monthly collection figures on line 5 and, (2) in "Total" column, by subtracting the figure on line 4 from the figure on line 3.

Exhibit 69

	JAN.	FEB.	MAR.	APR.	MAY	JUNE
DEPRECIATION						
Manufacturing Expenses	800	800	800	800	800	800
Sales Expenses	50	50	50	50	50	50
General & Administrative Expenses	15	15	15	15	15	15
TOTAL	865	865	865	865	865	865

Exhibit 70

(1.) plus (2.) equals (3.) *less (5.)* equals "4."
(100 plus 70 gives 170, less 120, equals *50)*

To view the appropriate calculations see Exhibits 68 and 69. The process is illustrated in two steps, for simplification. The results from Exhibit 69 were then posted to Exhibit 73, a summary sheet for both receipts and disbursements.

MISCELLANEOUS CASH RECEIPTS

Having just decided on the principal part of the cash flow, next we ask ourselves, "What *other* sources do we have for cash?" Listed below are some examples of the *types* of such receipts:

—Rent for space
—Sale of scrap
—Sale of equipment
—Miscellaneous "other income"

In this case, it was decided there *are* no such items, so none has to be considered.

NONCASH COSTS AND EXPENSES

There are certain costs and expenses that have an unusual quality in common: they do *not,* directly, involve the payment of *cash.* Included in this strange family of accounts are the following:

—Depreciation (of fixed assets)
—Amortization (of leasehold improvements, e.g.)
—Depletion (of natural resources—oil, etc.)
—Provision for bad debts

These accounts are being considered at this particular point for one reason: to measure

JULY	AUG.	SEPT.	OCT.	NOV.	DEC.	TOTAL
1200	1200	1200	1200	1200	1200	12000
100	100	100	100	150	150	1000
15	15	15	15	25	25	200
1315	1315	1315	1315	1375	1375	13200

Exhibit 70 (cont'd)

the debt repayment ability of a business, it has become fashionable to speak glibly of "cash flow," meaning the *combination* of (1) net profits and (2) depreciation—and other noncash charges (see Exhibit 30, p. 38). It would be just as logical to *subtract* these items from *disbursements,* but of course the net effect is the same.

In our case history, depreciation and bad debts are the only two candidates for consideration in this category. And management elected to treat bad debts as an actual cash outlay (the more conservative approach), leaving only depreciation to be dealt with. Depreciation occurs at three different points in the P. & L., so a work sheet was prepared to arrive at a total figure for each month (see Exhibit 70), and then the totals were posted to the R. & D. summary (Exhibit 73).

ADJUSTMENT OF CASH ACCOUNT

In this particular instance, the balance of the cash account at the end of last year was $13,100 (Exhibit 31, p. 40). The amount *estimated* for the cash account in a projection serves several needs. . . . First, it must be a somewhat realistic sum, with reference to the amount of money that management has discovered—over a period of time—that it *needs* to maintain in the checking account "in order to sleep nights." Second, it must be no greater than really necessary, because "efficiency is the name of the game," and it hasn't been fashionable to keep relatively unnecessary large balances at the bank for many years. In the third place, when establishing this figure, management should recognize that the bankers who will look at the finished projection are going to pay particular attention to the item: you are talking about their *product.* Finally, in a pinch management *knows* from experience that it *can* operate with a "zero" cash book balance, or maybe even a sizable "book overdraft"—relying on "float" to keep the bank's books in the black. So there is an element of protection or "cushion" in the balance of the cash account.

Weighing all these factors, management decided here that it would project on the basis of maintaining a $5,000 bank balance. This means that the balance will *change* from $13,100 at the beginning of the first month in the projection period, to $5,000 at the end of the period, so that the difference ($8,100) will flow *into* the business as a "cash receipt" during the first month. Therefore an appropriate entry was made in the receipts portion of the R. & D. summary (Exhibit 73).

If things were the other way around, say, and the balance at the beginning was $1,000 and you wanted to predict $5,000, you would include a "cash adjustment" item in the *disbursements* section for the $4,000.

"CROSSFOOTING"

Next the receipts section of Exhibit 73 was "crossfooted" to make certain the entries all total up properly, and then attention was turned to the *other* side of the coin, disbursements.

DISBURSEMENTS VS. COSTS AND EXPENSES

Remember, in thinking about the *outgoing* part of cash flow—disbursements— that one should think through each item based on when the cash *must* go out, without regard to when the cost or expense arose as such.

PAYMENTS FOR PURCHASES

Going back to the P. & L. (Exhibit 65, p. 90), we move down from sales (already considered from a cash flow standpoint) to the *cost of goods sold* section. There, the first item that requires consideration is *purchases*. The records of the company are such that purchasing data for past periods is not readily available. Therefore management used, instead of purchasing figures, "materials used" figures to study the past relationships between materials and *accounts payable*. (See Exhibit 71.) The *Accounts Payable* aging (Exhibit 36, p. 44) was also reviewed.

RELATIONSHIP—MATERIAL USAGE TO ACCOUNTS PAYABLE

YEAR	I MATERIALS USED[a]	II ACCOUNTS PAYABLE[b]	III COL. II DIV. BY COL. I	IV COL. III × 360 DAYS[c]
1	$ 40,000	9,000	22.5%	81
2	80,000	18,000	22.5	81
3	121,000	21,000	17.4	63
4	160,000	28,000	17.5	63
5	183,000	33,000	18.0	65

[a]From Exhibit 11.
[b]From Exhibit 1.
[c]Yields "days of material usage in accounts payable."

Exhibit 71

After concluding that it has been missing a substantial amount of discounts (somebody came up with an estimate of $2,500 for last year), management decided to assume—at this stage of the projection—that in future *all* bills, including particularly purchases, would be paid on a "30-day basis." That is, January purchases would be paid for in February, etc. The related calculations were worked up in the usual schedule basis (see Exhibit 72) and the resulting *payment* figures were posted to the R. & D. summary (Exhibit 73).

PAYMENTS FOR PURCHASES

	PURCHASES[a]	SCHEDULED PAYMENTS[b]
January	$ 29,744	——
February	29,744	29,744
March	33,462	29,744
April	33,462	33,462
May	37,180	33,462
June	22,308	37,180
July	22,308	22,308
August	33,462	22,308
September	37,180	33,462
October	37,180	37,180
November	29,744	37,180
December	26,026	29,744
TOTAL	$371,800	$345,774

[a]From Exhibit 50.
[b]Based on paying for January purchases in February, etc. (one month lag).

Exhibit 72

PAYMENTS FOR LABOR

Going on down the P. & L. checklist, next we encounter the labor figures. In practice, there would always be a certain amount of *un*paid labor costs, because it takes time to prepare a payroll, and there is usually *some* lag. Also, at month end there almost always would be some accrued labor, no matter how current the payroll.

Management decided to ignore any carryover factor, and to simply assume that *labor* is paid out in the *same* month the cost is incurred. So, all that is necessary is to go back to the P. & L. (Exhibit 65, p. 90) and get the monthly Labor figures, then post them to the R. & D. summary (Exhibit 73).

PAYMENTS FOR MANUFACTURING EXPENSES

Manufacturing expenses, next on the list, includes *some* items that would normally create payables—for example, "Repairs and Maintenance," "Supplies," and "Payroll Taxes."

SUMMARY—RECEIPTS

	JAN.	FEB.	MAR.	APR.	MAY
CASH RECEIPTS					
1. Collection—Accounts Receivable	27,213	49,302	64,350	85,734	33,462
2. Depreciation	865	865	865	865	865
3. Adj.—Cash Account	8,100	——	——	——	——
TOTAL	36,178	50,167	65,215	86,599	34,327
CASH DISBURSEMENTS					
4. Payments for Purchases	——	29,744	29,744	33,462	33,462
5. Payments for Labor	20,160	20,160	23,040	23,040	23,040
6. Payments for Mfg. Exp.	7,620	7,620	9,620	8,920	7,020
7. Payments for Expenses	8,045	8,245	8,545	9,145	9,570
8. Other Income—Other Charges (Net)	250	250	250	250	250
9. Payments for New Fixed Assets	——	——	——	——	——
10. Payment of Accounts Payable	33,000	——	——	——	——
11. Payment of N.P.—Bank	88,000	——	——	——	——
12. Payments on Notes & Contracts	916	916	916	916	917
13. Payments on Real Estate Mtge.	416	416	416	416	417
14. Payments on Income Taxes	——	——	12,800	——	——
TOTAL	158,407	67,351	85,331	76,149	74,676

Exhibit 73

For the sake of simplicity and conservatism, however, management decided to assume that all manufacturing expenses are paid for in the same month incurred. So once again all that is involved is going back to the P. & L. (Exhibit 65) for the manufacturing expense figures, and then posting them to the R. & D. summary (Exhibit 73).

PAYMENTS FOR EXPENSES

Again, when the two categories of expenses were analyzed, numerous items were discovered which have—or could have—a delay factor as to payment:

Advertising   Real Estate Taxes
Office Supplies & Stationery   Collection Expense
Telephone   Dues & Subscriptions
Professional Services   Interest
Insurance—General   Utilities
Insurance—Employee Hospitalization   Repairs and Maintenance
Personal Property Taxes

Once again, however, both because it is simpler and because it is more conservative to do so, management elected to treat *all* expenses as paid in the same month incurred.

AND DISBURSEMENTS

JUNE	JULY	AUG.	SEPT.	OCT.	NOV.	DEC.	TOTAL
41,382	49,302	57,222	58,905	93,357	73,953	93,357	727,539
865	1,315	1,315	1,315	1,315	1,375	1,375	13,200
——	——	——	——	——	——	——	8,100
42,247	50,617	58,537	60,220	94,672	75,328	94,732	748,839
37,180	22,308	22,308	33,462	37,180	37,180	29,744	345,774
23,040	23,040	25,920	25,920	25,920	25,920	28,800	288,000
6,920	7,820	8,132	8,232	8,232	8,532	8,532	97,200
9,820	10,070	11,620	11,930	12,630	12,990	13,190	125,800
250	250	250	250	250	250	250	3,000
——	54,000	——	——	——	7,200	——	61,200
——	——	——	——	——	——	——	33,000
——	——	——	——	——	——	——	88,000
917	917	917	917	917	917	917	11,000
417	417	417	417	417	417	417	5,000
——	——	——	——	——	——	——	12,800
78,544	118,822	69,564	81,128	85,546	93,406	81,850	1,070,774

Exhibit 73 (cont'd)

The figures for the total of expenses were taken from the P. & L. (Exhibit 65) and posted to the R. & D. summary (Exhibit 73).

OTHER INCOME—(OTHER CHARGES)—NET

This item management also considered as "to be paid out in cash the same month as incurred"—so the P. & L. figures were simply posted to the R. & D. summary (Exhibit 73).

PAYMENTS FOR NEW FIXED ASSETS

Unless a company is in an extremely liquid condition (which in our case, is *not* true), it is almost customary to *finance* sizable additions to fixed assets by some means. We may suppose management is aware of this generally accepted treatment, and is considering various methods of financing the additions planned for the forecast year; in fact, it may even be considering leasing.

First, management considered showing cash going out on these new purchases based on a 10 percent down payment and then appropriate monthly payments, assuming a four- or five-year program. "But we may have to *refinance all* of our fixed assets," management noted, and finally decided to forecast on the basis of paying 100 percent cash for the fixed additions—the idea and the effect being to *include* the problem of how to pay for them *along with* the problem of financing the *overall* program for the year ahead.

Accordingly, the planned additions:

$54,000—July
$ 7,200—Nov.

were posted to the R. & D. summary (Exhibit 73).

PAYMENT OF ACCOUNTS PAYABLE

The condition of the existing payables was considered (aging, Exhibit 36, p. 44), and then the alternatives weighed, from paying them all promptly to "stringing them out as long as possible." Finally, in a wish to "be conservative" and let the "overall need" include whatever stress might be involved in getting completely current with the trade, management decided to pay, in January, all of the accounts payable owing at the end of December. Accordingly, the $33,000 owing at December 31 (Exhibit 31, p. 40) was posted to the "January" column in the disbursements part of the R. & D. summary (Exhibit 73).

PAYMENT OF NOTES PAYABLE-BANK

The bank had been very cooperative, so far, in helping the company finance its operations. However, it expressed some concern about the increasing *amount* of borrowing required, and also the inability of the company to "clean up" (pay off) its debt for 30 or 60 days each year. At this juncture, the bank was *not* aware of management's aggressive plans (62 percent increase in sales, etc.) for the year ahead. And, indeed, management itself, right now, doesn't really have too much of an idea just what the company's financing needs are going to be in the year ahead.

Pending the completion of this projection effort, which is supposed to clarify the company's financial requirements during the projection period, management decided to assume that *some* kind of *re*financing *would* be required (either with the bank, with a commercial finance company, or "someplace"), and that the *existing* bank debt ($88,000, Exhibit 31) would have to be paid off and made a part of any new program. Therefore the $88,000 bank loan is shown as being paid in January on the R. & D. summary (Exhibit 73).

PAYMENTS ON NOTES AND CONTRACTS

The installment debt was reviewed in some detail in Chapter 11, when interest costs were estimated. Management noted that equipment notes and contract payments are estimated to run $11,255—including *both* interest and principal, and decided to use $11,000, spread out evenly over the year, on the R. & D. summary (Exhibit 73).

Just *after* the above entry had been made on the R. & D., the Office Manager pointed out that "it is wrong to use the $11,000 figure; the *interest* portion of the payments is *already* shown, in expenses, as cash flow out: here we should only show the *principal* portion of the payments." Management finally agreed with the Office Manager but decided to leave the entry on the R. & D. summary as originally made: "the difference is only about $3,000 for the year—leave it with the *larger* figure in there; the way this thing is shaping up, I have a hunch we'll be coming *back* to rectify a lot of these assumptions anyway, and this way we are, if anything, *exaggerating* our needs—being conservative. Right now, I want to lean that way."

PAYMENTS ON REAL ESTATE MORTGAGE

In projecting the real estate mortgage payments, management agreed, without much discussion, to show in the R. & D. summary only the *principal* portion of projected payments (see Chapter 11 and Exhibit 73).

PAYMENTS ON INCOME TAXES

Payments on income taxes relating to earnings during the *forecast* year are not due until March 15 of the *following* year. The $12,300 liability for *last* year's taxes, however, fell due in March *of* the projection period—and was so posted (see Exhibit 31 and Exhibit 73).

"CROSSFOOTING"

The income tax payments are the last entry to be made, so the R. & D. summary was totaled up and proved out—"up and down and sideways."

Now, to see what the cash receipts and disbursements *mean*. . . .

13

Implications of Cash Flow

resource—. . . 5. a source of strength or ability within oneself . . . 6. ability to deal promptly and effectively with problems, difficulties, etc.; resourcefulness.

—page 1211, *Webster's New World Dictionary, 2d College Ed.,* World Publishing Company, 1970

RECEIPTS vs. DISBURSEMENTS

As SOON AS THE R. & D. SUMMARY WAS TOTALED, MANAGEMENT pounced on the information (Exhibit 73) and quickly moved on to the next step: "Now, let's see what kind of a cash problem we've really got!"

Receipts and disbursements data from the R. & D. summary were posted to a new schedule, "Cumulative Loan Need" (Exhibit 74). Then this same schedule was completed and proved out (crossfooted).

"Well, what do we have? Let's *average* the end-of-month need figures, from Exhibit 74, and see what the load is we've got to carry."

END OF MONTH NEED[a]

January	$ 122,229
February	139,413
March	159,529
April	149,079
May	189,428
June	225,725
July	293,930
August	304,957
September	325,865
October	316,739
November	334,817
December	321,935
TOTAL	$2,883,646
AVERAGE[b]	$ 240,304

[a]From Exhibit 74.
[b]Total divided by 12.

Management's first reaction? Raised eyebrows, and a furrowed brow . . .

"Those are *pretty* sizable figures. Let's go back, now, and compare them with the figures we played around with when we estimated *interest*."

1. Bank loan carried forward.	$88,000
2. Additional short-term borrowing, as originally estimated.	60,000
3. (1. plus 2.).	$148,000
4. Additional need as measured by "average need," above.	$240,304

"Wow! *ONLY* almost $100,000 *more!* OK, what we're trying to do may be *impossible* —who knows? But just to see how *much* of a hole this puts in our program, let's figure the *interest* cost, compared with what we allowed for."

1. $240,304 at 8%	$19,224
2. $ 88,000 at 8%	$ 7,040
3. $ 60,000 at 8%	4,800
4. (2 plus 3)	$11,840
5. "Additional interest required" (1. less 4.)	$ 7,834

In other words, management was thinking, how realistic does our *profit* picture look *now?* And, with the "need figures" running so high, it might be necessary to borrow *all* of the needs from a finance company at relatively *high rates* (?15 percent). . . .

1. Profit *before* income taxes, per P. & L. (Exhibit 65).	$43,200
2. Less added interest "at worst" ($240,304 at 15% equals $36,046, less $11,840 already provided for).	$24,206
3. "Adjusted net profit before taxes" (1. less 2.).	$18,994

"Well, that would be a pitiful result for all the extra effort spelled out for the months ahead. But at least it looks *possible*. To tell you the truth, what is *really* worrying *me*

CUMULATIVE LOAN NEED

	JAN.	FEB.	MAR.	APR.	MAY	JUNE	JULY	AUG.	SEPT.	OCT.	NOV.	DEC.	TOTAL
Receipts	36,178	50,167	65,215	86,599	34,327	42,247	50,617	58,537	60,220	94,672	75,328	94,732	748,839
Disbursements	158,407	67,351	85,331	76,149	74,676	78,544	118,822	69,564	81,128	85,546	93,406	81,850	1,070,774
Rec. Plus Disb.				10,450						9,126		12,882	32,458
Disb. Plus Rec.	122,229	17,184	20,116		40,349	36,297	68,205	11,027	20,908		18,078		355,393
Cumulative Total	122,229	139,413	159,529	149,079	189,428	225,725	293,930	304,957	325,865	316,739	334,817	321,935	321,935

Exhibit 74

ACCOUNTS RECEIVABLE AS COLLATERAL

	JAN.	FEB.	MAR.	APR.	MAY	JUNE	JULY	AUG.	SEPT.	OCT.	NOV.	DEC.
1. Balance, Accts. Rec., End of Mo.[a]	107,217	122,265	122,265	77,121	92,169	107,217	122,265	137,313	165,528	152,361	165,528	152,361
2. (Less Estimated Old Accounts)[b]	(10,722)	(12,227)	(12,227)	(7,712)	(9,217)	(10,722)	(12,227)	(13,731)	(16,553)	(15,236)	(16,553)	(15,236)
3. "Eligible Accounts" (1.)–(2.)	96,495	110,038	110,038	69,409	82,952	96,495	110,038	123,582	148,975	137,125	148,975	137,125
4. Possible Loan (3 at 75%)	72,372	82,529	82,529	52,057	62,214	72,372	82,529	92,687	111,732	102,844	111,732	102,844

[a]From Exhibit 67.
[b]Est. at 10%.

Exhibit 75

right now is the problem of getting *somebody* to loan us over *$300,000* toward the end of the year—almost *four times* what we *have* been able to get at the bank. . . ."

Spurred by management's reactions (above), the Office Manager and the others involved in the projection effort began to express doubts, raise questions, and throw out comments. Finally, the President got up from his desk and said, "Look: we've come to a sort of logical stopping place here, now that we know something, at least, about the *financing problems* that will confront us. It's late, and it's Friday. I tell you what: let's sleep on it, then come down here to the plant tomorrow. It will be quiet around here then, and we'll have a so-called brainstorming session: we'll all get our ideas down on paper, and dig into the alternatives one by one, see just what the right answers *are*. In the meantime, take it from me: we *are* going to go forward as we've planned—one way or another! So get a good rest, and come back in the morning with your thinking caps on. . . ."

SOLVING THE FINANCIAL PROBLEM

Next morning, the "projection crew" gathered at the plant, as planned. The President led off with some thoughts that had occurred to him since the group disbanded the previous afternoon: "I think that we *do* want to "brainstorm" this thing, but *first* I think we need to get the problem in sharper focus, and it occurs to me that there is a fairly easy way to do this. We are going to *have* to borrow a lot of money—that is for certain. But *on what?* Collateral, of course. So—what do we have to *offer* as collateral? *First,* in order of "quality" or liquidity(as the bank, or a finance company, will look at it) we have *receivables*. Second, we have *inventory:* raw material inventory and then finished goods inventory. What I suggest, therefore, is that—*before* we go ahead and organize our thinking on how we can finance this next year—it is sensible to see how *much* of our problem might be solved by receivable and inventory financing, which we *know* (or *think*) is a "way out" for at least *some* of the need.

RECEIVABLE FINANCING

Accordingly, attention turned next to an analysis of accounts receivable as collateral. It was decided to assume that 10 percent of the total receivables would, at any time, be considered ineligible for financing, either because the accounts were relatively old or due from companies with poor credit ratings. Then, a calculation was made to see how much might be borrowed on the remaining receivables (see Exhibit 75).

Immediately, with a pretty good idea of the support available from receivables collateral, interest next went to the question, "What is *left* to be financed?" The answer to this question was obtained in schedule fashion as shown in Exhibit 76.

INVENTORY FINANCING

Raw materials inventory, the next most liquid asset, was discussed as to the degree of reliance a lender might place on such an asset. Management concluded that

LOAN NEED—OTHER THAN RECEIVABLES

	JAN.	FEB.	MAR.	APR.	MAY	JUNE	JULY	AUG.	SEPT.	OCT.	NOV.	DEC.
1. Total Need[a]	122,229	139,413	159,529	149,079	189,428	225,725	293,930	304,957	325,865	316,739	334,817	321,935
2. 75% Loan, Receivables[b]	72,372	82,529	82,529	52,057	62,214	72,372	82,529	92,687	111,732	102,844	111,732	102,844
3. Need—*Other* Collateral (1.)−(2.)	49,857	56,884	77,000	97,022	127,214	153,353	211,401	212,270	214,133	213,895	223,085	219,091

[b]From Exhibit 75.
[a]From Exhibit 74.

Exhibit 76

RAW MATERIAL INVENTORY AS COLLATERAL

	JAN.	FEB.	MAR.	APR.	MAY	JUNE	JULY	AUG.	SEPT.	OCT.	NOV.	DEC.
1. Raw Material Inventory, End of Month[a]	52,308	55,268	61,946	65,276	72,324	61,152	63,372	76,746	83,794	87,494	83,758	83,000
2. Possible Loan (1. at 40%)	20,923	22,107	24,778	26,110	28,930	24,461	25,349	30,698	33,518	34,998	33,503	33,200

[a]From Exhibit 52.

Exhibit 77

even on a "quick-sale" basis it could get about 70–75 percent on the dollar (of costs) for these goods, and that "it should be possible to persuade a lender to advance *40 percent*." So next a calculation was made as to what this would mean, in terms of a loan (see Exhibit 77).

Finished goods, management felt, could be disposed of easily, at any time, at cost, or at least for about *80 percent*. Based on this line of reasoning it was assumed that a lender would be willing to advance *60 percent* (see Exhibit 78).

SOLVING THE "EXCESS" NEED

"So, where does *this* leave us?" The calculations as to receivable and inventory financing were summarized (see Exhibit 79). "Clearly, we are left with quite a problem for ten months of the year. *Now* I think we are ready for our 'brainstorming' session." With the Office Manager presiding at the blackboard, they began to react to management's question: "OK—*how* shall we lick this remaining financing problem?"

By noontime the blackboard was covered with thoughts, listed by management in the order it wanted to consider them, as follows:

1. *Additional* loan on existing equipment.
2. Borrow heavily on *newly* acquired equipment.
3. *Lease* new equipment.
4. Obtain *second* mortgage on factory building.
5. Collect receivables *faster*.
6. *Raise* prices on products.
7. Improve *turn* on inventory.
8. Improve gross profit *percentage*.
9. Obtain *extended* terms from suppliers, pay accounts payable slower.
10. Borrow *higher* percentages on receivables and inventory.
11. Sell *debentures* to private investors.
12. Take in a *partner;* sell capital stock.
13. *Lower* objectives for this year.
14. Negotiate a *sale-leaseback* arrangement for fixed assets (plant and/or equipment).
15. *Cut* salaries.
16. Obtain *S.B.A.* loan on fixed assets.
17. Obtain S.B.I.C. loan.

That afternoon the process of considering these various alternatives began. The first alternative to be considered was to borrow *more* on equipment.

Additional Loan on Existing Equipment

The present situation was as follows, regarding equipment:

Cost	$93,300
Reserve for depreciation	54,100
Net book value	$39,200
Total owed	$38,300

FINISHED GOODS INVENTORY AS COLLATERAL

	JAN.	FEB.	MAR.	APR.	MAY	JUNE	JULY	AUG.	SEPT.	OCT.	NOV.	DEC.
1. Fin. Gds. Inv., End of Mo.[a]	55,387	57,900	65,293	93,999	114,584	132,195	131,092	126,960	121,306	124,444	122,438	122,100
2. Possible Loan (1. at 60%)	33,232	34,740	39,176	56,399	68,750	79,317	78,655	76,176	72,784	74,666	73,463	73,260

[a]From Exhibit 61.

Exhibit 78

LOAN NEED—OTHER THAN RECEIVABLES AND INVENTORY

	JAN.	FEB.	MAR.	APR.	MAY	JUNE	JULY	AUG.	SEPT.	OCT.	NOV.	DEC.
1. Need—*Other* Than Receivables[a]	49,857	56,884	77,000	97,022	127,214	153,353	211,401	212,270	214,133	213,895	223,085	219,091
2. (Less—40% Loan on R. M. Inv.)[b]	20,923	22,107	24,778	26,110	28,930	24,461	25,349	30,698	33,518	34,998	33,503	33,200
3. Need—*Other* Than Rec., R. M. Inv. (1.)−(2.)	28,934	34,777	52,222	70,912	98,284	128,892	186,052	181,572	180,615	178,897	189,582	185,891
4. (Less—60% Loan on Fin. Gds. Inv.)[c]	33,232	34,740	39,176	56,399	68,750	79,317	78,655	76,176	72,784	74,666	73,463	73,260
5. Need—*Other* Than Rec., R. M. Inv., & Fin. Gds. Inv. (3.)−(4.)	(4,298)	37	13,046	14,513	29,534	49,575	107,397	105,396	107,831	104,231	116,119	112,631

[a]From Exhibit 76.
[b]From Exhibit 77.
[c]From Exhibit 78.

Exhibit 79

Although accelerated depreciation methods were used, and management believed the equipment would sell—even on a "quick-sale" basis—for more like $60,000 than the $39,200 net book value—even on this basis a "loan value" of only about $48,000 would be indicated (80 percent basis). There would be a penalty in paying off most of the contracts, so this did *not* appear to be a very likely or economical source for funds.

Borrow on New Equipment?

In the projection, cash was provided for new purchases: $54,000 in July and $7,800 in November. Management believes it can borrow on a supplier-provided program 90 percent on these new purchases on a four-year basis with 7 percent add-on interest, so an entry was made on a new "additional needs" work sheet (Exhibit 80), based on the following:

	JULY	NOVEMBER
Purchase	$54,000	$7,200
Down payment	5,400	720
Cash advantage	$48,600	$6,480

Monthly payments would be approximately as shown below:

$48,600.00	$6,480.00
7%	7%
$ 3,402.00	$ 453.60
4 years	4 years
$13,608.00 Total interest	$1,814.40 Total interest
48,600.00 Principal	6,480.00 Principal
$62,208.00 Total debt	$8,294.40 Total debt
$ 1,296.00[a] Monthly payment	$ 172.80[b] Monthly payment

[a]Total debt divided by 48 months; $1,012.50 principal, $283.50 interest.
[b]Total debt divided by 48 months; $135.00 principal, $37.80 interest.

Lease New Equipment?

Based on information obtained from a leasing company representative when he called several months ago, there is reason to think that new machinery *could* be leased on the basis of 100 percent of the purchase price, at what would approximate 8 percent add-on interest, for a period of five years, with three lease payments being made in advance. Thus the following cash-flow advantages would appear an appropriate basis for figuring:

	JULY	NOVEMBER
Cost	$54,000.00	$ 7,200.00
	8%	8%
	$ 4,320.00	$ 576.00
	5 years	5 years
	$21,600.00	$ 2,880.00
Principal	54,000.00	7,200.00
	75,600.00[a]	$10,080.00[a]
Monthly payment	$ 1,260.00	$ 168.00

[a]Divided by 60 months, yields monthly payment.

Based on the above, and on previous calculations made on a *loan* basis, the "cash advantage" (as against just paying 100 percent out for the purchase of the equipment, which was the basis used in the projection) of the *lease* basis would be as follows, for the projection year:

CASH REQUIREMENTS

	JULY	AUG.	SEPT.	OCT.	NOV.	DEC.	TOTAL
1. *Cash* purchase	54,000	——	——	——	7,200	——	61,200
2. *Loan* basis	5,400[a]	1,296	1,296	1,296	1,296	1,296	12,773
					720[a]	173	
3. *Lease* basis	3,780[b]	1,260	1,260	1,260	1,260	1,260	10,752
					504[b]	168	

[a]Downpayment of 10%; other figures are total *principal* and *interest* portions of monthly payments.
[b]Three payments in advance.

The lease basis, then, would only provide a $2,021 advantage during the forecast period, and this advantage (which amounts to only about 15 percent) would be on an expensive basis, so management decided *not* to consider the lease approach.

Second Mortgage on Building?

When the existing mortgage was taken out, it amounted to 69 percent of the *cost* of the land and building ($85,000). The balance of the mortgage (which was originally $59,000) is now $54,000. The insurance company that made the mortgage is understood to make its loans in the basis of *60 percent* of value, which would indicate a value of $98,000. Thus it might be reasoned that there is a "gap" of *$44,000* between the value of the land and building and the mortgage balance ("it won't have depreciated much if any in the less than two years since it was built; may actually have *appreciated* some").

Management checked around several weeks ago and found out that there were two local firms making second mortgages on factory buildings, and that a $25,000 second mortgage, on a five-year basis, at a rate of about 14 percent, should be available.

WORK SHEET—ADDITIONAL NEED

	JAN.	FEB.	MAR.	APR.	MAY	JUNE	JULY	AUG.	SEPT.	OCT.	NOV.	DEC.
1. "Additional Need"[a]	(4,298)	37	13,046	14,513	29,534	49,575	107,397	105,396	107,831	104,231	116,119	112,631
2. Borrow on New Equipment[b]	—	—	—	—	—	—	(48,600)	(48,600)	(48,600)	(48,600)	(48,600)	(48,600)
											(6,480)	(6,480)
								1,013	2,026	3,039	4,052	5,065
												135
3. Second Mortgage on Bldg.	(25,000)	(25,000)	(25,000)	(25,000)	(25,000)	(25,000)	(25,000)	(25,000)	(25,000)	(25,000)	(25,000)	(25,000)
		400[c]	800	1,200	1,600	2,000	2,400	2,800	3,200	3,600	4,000	4,400
4. Payables on 60-Day Basis		(29,744)	(29,744)	(33,462)	(33,462)	(37,180)	(22,308)	(22,308)	(33,462)	(37,180)	(37,180)	(29,744)
5. Borrow Heavier on Collateral[d]	(12,823)	(13,922)	(14,959)	(14,696)	(17,108)	(17,548)	(18,392)	(20,201)	(21,892)	(21,827)	(21,944)	(21,261)
TOTAL	(42,121)[e]	(68,229)	(55,857)	(57,445)	(44,436)	(32,153)	(4,503)	(7,400)	(15,897)	(21,737)	(15,033)	(8,854)

[a]From Exhibit 79—"need *after* borrowing 75% on eligible receivables, 40% on raw material inventory, and 60% on finished goods inventory."
[b]48,600 borrowed July, $6,480 in November; less payments (*principal* portion of $1,013 beginning in August and $135 beginning in December).
[c]Total payment each month would scale *down* from approximately $700.00 the first month ($400 principal, $300 interest), assuming level fixed principal payments—so here $400 of principal used.
[d]From Column VII, Exhibit 82.
[e]Figures in brackets, represent needs "provided" in *excess* of indicated requirements.

Exhibit 80

Tentatively, management decided to obtain such a loan, so its impact on cash flow was posted to Exhibit 80, the work sheet for "additional needs."

Principal	$25,000.00
	14%
Interest, 1 year	$ 3,500.00
Interest, first month	$ 291.67

Equal monthly principal payments (*if* payments were *fixed* on principal, *plus* interest each month) would be $416.67

Collect Receivables Faster?

Management has checked, and believes that a *goal* of 45 days' sales in receivables is realistic (versus *57* days used in the projection). During the forecast period net sales are projected to *average* about $67,000 per month (or about $2,233 per *day,* 30-day basis). So an improvement from 57 to 45 days would "free up" *$26,796* ($2,233 times 12 days).

After considering this aspect of cash flow, management decided it would definitely work harder during the coming year to *achieve* the goal, but that it would prefer *not* to "count these chickens until the eggs hatched."

Raise Prices?

When it was pointed out that even a "modest" increase in prices, like 3 percent, would yield over $24,000—*almost* as much as the net *profit* for the forecast year, management agreed that this possibility should definitely be explored further. For planning purposes, however, it was concluded that it would *not* be prudent to make any assumptions about raising prices at the time.

Improve Inventory Turn?

Most of those present at this "projection session" had agreed quickly that this should be a fruitful avenue for some improvement. "First, let's review what we have *done* on this score," suggested the Office Manager. So they looked back to see what the "days' cost of goods sold in inventory" figures *had* been running (Exhibit 7, p. 23). Then the figures as of the *end* of the projection year were used to compute the same ratio:

R. M. inventory	$ 83,000[a]
WIP inventory	$ 27,000[a]
F. G. inventory	$122,100[a]
I. Total	$232,100

II. 232,100 divided by C. of G. S. (629,900), gives—.37, times 360 days gives—*133* days.

---

[a]From Exhibit 65.

This compared with *actual* performance over the past five years as follows:

YEAR	DAYS' C. OF G. S. IN INVENTORY[a]	
1	155	
2	104	
3	101	
4	101	
5	97	
PROJECTED	133	(above)

[a]From Exhibit 7.

"Percentage-wise, we're planning on being 37 percent *less* efficient this year. Can't we do better than *that?*" said the factory foreman. Which raised the next question, "If we were only *10 percent* less efficient, say, to allow for some elbowroom (with new products involved, and such a big increase in sales), what would it mean in *dollars?*"

1. Last year	97 days'	
2. 10% more	10 days'	
3. (1. + 2.)	107 days'	
4. One days' C. of G. S. (629,900 divided by 360 days)	$ 1,750	
5. 107 days' (4. × 3.)	$187,250	
6. Inventory, end of projection year	$232,100	
7. "Gain" or advantage (6. − 5.)	$ 44,850	

As an *indication* of whether or not too much inventory had been projected, the above would seem to support the proposition that there are adjustments—of a worthwhile size—that could be made. In any event, the above analysis prompted more of the same. . . .

Next, attention turned to raw materials inventory. The question, "Couldn't—shouldn't—we be perfectly safe in carrying only a month and a half's needs ahead of raw materials?" To compare these relationships a schedule was prepared (see Exhibit 81). Viewing the *past* relationships, at least on a year-end basis, the raw materials inventory in the projection appears "in line." *But,* at 89 days' needs—not *45 days'* (which would represent a month and a half's requirements).

At this point management interjected, "Look: we're losing sight of something here; when we started out, earlier in the projection, we *purposely* forecast on the basis of *$900,000* of *production.* All of you may not have known or realized why, but the principal reason was that we are projecting a dramatic increase in the sales of Product D and that we'll do $150,000 worth of sales with our newest product, Product E. And we want to be able to *fill* these orders *quickly,* with no back ordering. So—for right now, at least—I would like to *drop* further consideration of adjustments in inventory as a way of cutting our loan requirements. If we *must,* I *know* we *can* cut some in both raw and finished, but this year I would rather *plan* on having plenty on hand."

RELATIONSHIP—RAW MATERIALS USAGE AND INVENTORY

YEAR	I MATERIALS USED[a]	II RAW MATERIALS INVENTORY[b]	III COL. II DIV. BY COL. I	IV COL. III × 360 DAYS[c]
1	$ 40,000	$15,000	37.50%	135 days
2	80,000	23,000	28.75	104
3	121,000	28,000	23.14	83
4	160,000	38,000	23.75	86
5	183,000	46,000	25.14	91
6 (?)	$334,800[d]	$83,000[d]	24.79%	89 days

[a]From Exhibit 11.
[b]From Exhibit 1.
[c]Yields "Days' of Material Usage in Raw Material Usage in Inventory."
[d]From Exhibit 53.

Exhibit 81

Improve Gross Profit Percentage?

Right at the outset of the discussion of this item it was agreed there were two ways to accomplish this: higher prices (which possibility was already considered, and rejected) or lower costs. So attention turned to a review of the pertinent history, with emphasis on costs:

YEAR	GROSS PROFIT— % TO SALES	MATERIAL COST— % TO SALES	LABOR COSTS— % TO SALES	MFG. EXPENSES— % TO SALES
1	19.0%[a]	40.0%[b]	30.0%[c]	8.0%[d]
2	21.5%[a]	40.0%[b]	30.5%[c]	14.2%[d]
3	23.0%[a]	40.5%[b]	30.0%[c]	7.9%[d]
4	19.0%[a]	40.0%[b]	35.3%[c]	6.0%[d]
5	23.6%[a]	36.5%[b]	31.3%[c]	10.3%[d]
PROJECTED	21.2%[e]	41.3%[f]	35.6%[f]	12.0%[f]

[a]From Exhibit 18.
[b]From Exhibit 19.
[c]From Exhibit 20.
[d]From Exhibit 22.
[e]Calculated using Exhibit 65 figures (172,000 divided by 810,000).
[f]Calculated, using figures from Exhibit 65.

"As is always the case," said the President, "these statistics *look* impressive when you set them down in black and white. But before we get carried away, let me point out that in relating *costs* of manufacturing to *sales*—which is what we are doing— we are mixing apples and oranges. . . . See what I mean? No? OK, *add up* material, labor, and manufacturing expenses and you get *110.1 percent*—*more* than *100 percent,* you see; what is *not* considered here is the *increase* in finished goods inventory. Anyway, I want to leave the gross profit figure alone: I *know,* myself, we can *beat* the 21.2

percent figure. *I* think that with any luck, we'll average more like *25 percent* for the year, because we're almost certain to run close to *30 percent* as soon as we get our new machinery in. But you see, the only item we know to be cockeyed in our P. & L. is interest, and that, at $18,000, may be low by as much as $24,206. Now, the way I figure is this: we can *make up* for this extra interest, first, by cutting our borrowings, and thus their cost, and secondly, by getting a *better* gross profit. For example, if we can get *2.0 percent* more—a 23.2 percent gross, compared to 23.6 percent for last year, so not an unreasonable result to expect—that's $16,200 of the $24,000 'extra interest.' In any event, I want to *save* this plus factor, and for now, at least, not consider it as a solution to our financing problem."

Extended Terms from Suppliers?

It will be recalled that the basis used for paying suppliers was "a 30-day" one. Now that it has considered just how *much* additional borrowing expanded activity will entail, management has said, "If we are going to do things like get a second mortgage, why, let's reexamine our premises as to trade debt; see just how *much* of this 'free' money we can get, if we set our minds to it!"

After some analysis of purchases, with special attention to terms and discounts extended, as *well* as management's "feel" as to the supplier companies' *attitudes*, there was a general agreement that although it *might* be possible to do even *better* than this, that "for sure" it would be possible to get *60*-day terms from suppliers representing about 40 percent of purchases, and *90*-day terms from suppliers representing about 30 percent of purchases—the remaining 30 percent being on a 30-day basis.

To determine just what this "pattern" of payments would mean, the following "model" was prepared:

PERIOD	PURCHASES	1	2	3	4	5	6	7	LATER
1	1,000	—	300	400	300				
2	1,000	—	—	300	400	300			
3	1,000	—	—	—	300	400	300		
4	1,000	—	—	—	—	300	400	300	
5	1,000	—	—	—	—	—	300	400	300
6	1,000	—	—	—	—	—	—	300	700
TOTAL PAID PER MONTH		300	700	1,000	1,000	1,000	1,000	1,000	

Based on the above "pattern," payables would show end-of-month balances as shown below:

	PERIODS						
	1	2	3	4	5	6	7
Beg. Balance	0	1,000	1,700	2,000	2,000	2,000	2,000
Purchases	1,000	1,000	1,000	1,000	1,000	1,000	1,000
Subtotal	1,000	2,000	2,700	3,000	3,000	3,000	3,000
(Payments)	0	300	700	1,000	1,000	1,000	1,000
End Balance	1,000	1,700	2,000	2,000	2,000	2,000	2,000

It was noted, then, that with purchases of $1,000 per month, paying 30 percent on a 30-day basis, 40 percent on a 60-day basis, and 30 percent on a 90-day basis, payables leveled off at *$2,000*—or, to phrase it in a *different* way, as "60 days" of purchases.

Management noted that by using such a basis for forecasting that there *still* would be no reliance on the "deferral potential" in the *expense* part of the P. & L., so decided to *use* 60 days as a projection factor, instead of the *30*-day basis used originally.

The "improvement" in the cash flow was determined below, then posted to line 4 on Exhibit 80.

	PURCHASES[a]	PAYMENTS ON PUR., 30-DAY BASIS[a]	PAYMENTS ON PUR., 60-DAY BASIS	ADVANTAGE (DIS.—ADV.)
January	$29,744	——	——	——
February	29,744	29,744	——	29,744
March	33,462	29,744	29,744	——
April	33,462	33,462	29,744	3,718
May	37,180	33,462	33,462	——
June	22,308	37,180	33,462	3,718
July	22,308	22,308	37,180	(14,872)
August	33,462	22,308	22,308	——
September	37,180	33,462	22,308	11,154
October	37,180	37,180	33,462	3,718
November	29,744	37,180	37,180	——
December	26,026	29,744	37,180	(7,436)

[a]From Exhibit 72.

Borrow More on Collateral?

Management used 75 percent for receivables, 40 percent on raw materials, and 60 percent on finished goods, because these were the relationships suggested as "most likely" when the matters were originally discussed with a representative of a commercial finance company. Management talked with the finance company again, and explained that it looked like *more* reliance must be placed on collateral—"What are the *outside* limits?" It was made clear that no commitment could be made until the finance company had sent its men over to make a detailed examination. The company said it "could probably go" to *80 percent* on receivables (up 5 percent), *50 percent* on raw (up 10 percent) and 65 percent (up 5 percent) on finished goods, "*If* we took a second mortgage on your equipment and your personal guaranty."

Using the new percentages, management calculated the relief that would be provided. The calculations are shown on Exhibit 82, and then posted to Exhibit 80.

Sell Debentures?

Last year the company's banker brought up this possibility, pointing out that he knew several small companies that were having some degree of success in selling

WORK SHEET—HEAVIER BORROWING

	I A/C RECEIVABLES NET OF INELIGIBLE ACCOUNTS[a]	II 5% OF COL. I[b]	III R. M. INVENTORY[c]	IV 10% OF COL. III[d]	V F. G. INVENTORY[e]	VI 5% OR COL. V[f]	VII TOTAL COLS. II, IV, VI
January	96,495	4,824	52,308	5,230	55,387	2,769	12,823
February	110,038	5,501	55,268	5,526	57,900	2,895	13,922
March	110,038	5,501	61,946	6,194	65,293	3,264	14,959
April	69,409	3,470	65,276	6,527	93,999	4,699	14,696
May	82,952	4,147	72,324	7,232	114,584	5,729	17,108
June	96,495	4,824	61,152	6,115	132,195	6,609	17,548
July	110,038	5,501	63,372	6,337	131,092	6,554	18,392
August	123,582	6,179	76,746	7,674	126,960	6,348	20,201
September	148,975	7,448	83,794	8,379	121,306	6,065	21,892
October	137,125	6,856	87,494	8,749	124,444	6,222	21,827
November	148,975	7,448	83,758	8,375	122,438	6,121	21,944
December	137,125	6,856	83,000	8,300	122,100	6,105	21,261

[a]From Exhibit 75.
[b]From 75% to 80%.
[c]From Exhibit 77.
[d]From 40% to 50%.
[e]From Exhibit 78.
[f]From 60% to 65%.

Exhibit 82

debentures (unsecured, long-term notes) with maturities up to five years at rates of 8, 9, and 10 percent.

Management said, "If it comes to it, I suppose we could try this route, but it would require us to file a detailed prospectus with the state securities people—and I don't like to make our figures public—and also, it takes a lot of time and effort; I would rather spend our time making money with our business. Let's not count on this as a solution."

Sell Capital Stock?

Here management cut the discussion short: "This company is *not* going to sell any stock—at least in the forseeable future."

Lower Objectives?

Again, management curtailed consideration: "Of course, like one banker we used to have always advised us, we can probably cut back and so conduct our affairs that we *don't* grow. But I am not at *all* sure such an unnatural route could be handled profitably, and I'm *positive* it's even more hazardous—in terms of the long-term future —than trying to rise and meet or fill our expanding markets. No, like I told you the other day: one way or the other, we're going ahead."

Sale—Leaseback?

It is known that one local manufacturer "solved his problems" by resorting to sale-leaseback a few years ago—only to find that when a plant addition was needed he had no way to work it out.

"Borrowing on my assets I don't mind, but ownership—and the advantage of long-term capital appreciation—I want to keep. So forget this alternative," said management.

Cut Salaries?

No one had much to say on this topic. Without *saying* anything, management *thought,* "The only change I can realistically make here is to forget the raise I have planned for myself later in the year, and I will forego it, when the time comes, *if* necessary."

All management *said* was, "It has always been part of our philosophy here that we all try to grow a little bit *together.* As I have perhaps mentioned to all of you at one time or another in private discussions, it is my *hope* that sometime ahead we will be in a position to put in a *profit sharing program;* if we can "cut the mustard" and make a good showing, meet and surpass our goals and financing problems, why this might be the year. Anyway, we won't move ahead very far cutting salaries. . . ."

S.B.A. Loan?

Several of those present were familiar with one situation or another where a company had obtained a loan from the government's Small Business Administration.

Advantages and disadvantages were discussed, until management interrupted: "We won't spend a lot of time weighing this alternative. As you have seen, it is our receivables and inventory that are really causing the trouble; on our fixed assets we can *get* pretty good financing. And, as I understand it, the S.B.A. principally makes loans on *fixed* assets; their programs just aren't geared to fluctuating receivables and inventory needs. Also, they tie you up so tight you can't breathe, and there is a lot of red tape involved. Then too, I just don't like the whole idea. So, unless we are *really* destitute or one of you can show me some big advantage I'm not aware of, why, let's forget about the S.B.A."

S.B.I.C. Loan?

A year or so ago management attended a seminar on small-business-investment-companies ("S.B.I.C.'s"). "As I understand it, you get unsecured long-term debt but you give up equity, and—although there are probably exceptions—in general your company has to 'have a public stock market destiny' in order to get this kind of money. We are a long way from that type of situation now—so let's just add up that work sheet and see if we haven't already *solved* our problem!" said the President.

The work sheet (Exhibit 80) was rendered current, and sure enough, its totals indicated the problem *had* been "solved." It was suggested, however, that the calculations be *re*checked and the various proposed steps be presented in a somewhat more orthodox fashion; so a "reanalysis" was prepared.

"REANALYSIS" OF NEEDS

The "rechecking" or "reanalysis" of loan needs was begun by listing the *total* need originally determined by comparing monthly cash receipts and cash disbursements (see line 1, Exhibit 83). Next the need was adjusted by the amount of additional trade debt it is now assumed can be obtained (see lines 2 and 3, Exhibit 83).

Then, from the "adjusted need" figures the proceeds of the second mortgage and the relief provided by borrowing on the new equipment was subtracted (see lines 4 and 5, Exhibit 83), leaving the amount the company needed to borrow from the finance company and/or the bank (line 6). Finally, the required receivables-inventory loan was analyzed from the standpoint of collateral coverage (lines 7, 8, and 9). The *degree* of reliance required on finished goods inventory was computed (line 10), and it was noted that the maximum required was 62 percent in the month of July.

"OK," said the President. "Now I know what I wanted to know. Completing the projection—that is, getting proforma balance sheets for each month—should be pretty much of an accounting proposition, so we'll leave that in good hands," he said to the office-manager-accountant. . . .

REANALYSIS OF NEEDS

	JAN.	FEB.	MAR.	APR.	MAY	JUNE	JULY	AUG.	SEPT.	OCT.	NOV.	DEC.
1. Original need—cash receipts vs. cash disbursements[a]	122,229	139,413	159,529	149,079	189,428	225,725	293,930	304,957	325,865	316,739	334,817	321,935
2. Portion of need met by obtaining extended trade debt[b]	—	(29,744)	(29,744)	(33,462)	(33,462)	(37,180)	(22,308)	(22,308)	(33,462)	(37,180)	(37,180)	(29,744)
3. Adjusted need (1.)−(2.)	122,229	109,669	129,785	115,617	155,966	188,545	271,622	282,649	292,403	279,559	297,637	292,191
4. Portion of need met by obtaining second mortgage on factory building[c]	(25,000)	(24,600)	(24,200)	(23,800)	(23,400)	(23,000)	(22,600)	(22,200)	(21,800)	(21,400)	(21,000)	(20,600)
5. Portion of need met by borrowing on new equipment[d]	—	—	—	—	—	—	(48,600)	(47,587)	(46,574)	(45,561)	(44,548)	(43,535)
											(6,480)	(6,335)
6. Need to borrow on receivables and inventory from finance company and/or bank (3.)−(4.) and −(5.)	97,229	85,069	105,585	91,817	132,566	165,545	200,422	212,862	224,029	212,598	225,609	221,721
Collateral Coverage:												
7. Available on basis of 80% of eligible receivables[e]	77,196	88,030	88,030	55,527	66,361	77,196	88,030	98,866	119,180	109,700	119,180	109,700
8. Available on basis of 50% of raw material inventory[f]	26,154	27,634	30,973	32,638	36,162	30,576	31,686	38,373	41,897	43,747	41,879	41,500
9. Need to borrow on finished goods inventory (6.)−(7.)−(8.)	(612)	(30,595)	(13,418)	3,652	20,043	57,773	80,706	75,623	62,952	59,151	64,550	70,521
10. Percentage reliance needed on finished goods inventory[g]	0%	0%	0%	4%	18%	44%	62%	59%	52%	48%	53%	58%

[a]From Exhibit 74.
[b]From line 4, Exhibit 80.
[c]From line 3, Exhibit 80.
[d]From line 2, Exhibit 80.

[e]Line 3, Exhibit 75, times 80%.
[f]Line 1, Exhibit 77, times 50%.
[g]Line 9 as percent of Fin. Gds. Inventory, line 1, Exhibit 78.

Exhibit 83

14
Proforma Balance Sheets

From the viewpoint of the bank loaning officer . . . the balance sheet is probably the most important, and surely the most used of the . . . financial statements. . . .

—Page 177, *Practical Bank Credit,*
PROCHNOW AND FOULKE,
Prentice-Hall, Inc., 1950.

THE GOAL IN THIS CHAPTER IS SIMPLY TO DO WHATEVER IS NECESSARY to wind up with a figure for each balance sheet account, for each month-end during the projection period. Accordingly, all results are "posted" to Exhibit 84.

CASH

Earlier, in Chapter 12, it was decided to project cash at $5,000. Accordingly, this figure is used for the end-of-month balance throughout the projection period.

ACCOUNTS RECEIVABLE

The end-of-month balances for this account were previously calculated (in Exhibit 67). The figures calculated at that time were simply entered in the appropriate spaces on Exhibit 84.

As of the *end* of the month shown: **PROJECTED BALANCE**

	JAN.	FEB.	MAR.	APR.	MAY
Cash	5,000	5,000	5,000	5,000	5,000
Accounts Receivable	107,217	122,265	122,265	77,121	92,169
Inventory—Finished Goods	55,387	57,900	65,293	93,999	114,584
—Raw Materials	52,308	55,268	61,946	65,276	72,324
—Work in Process	10,500	12,000	13,500	15,000	16,500
CURRENT ASSETS	230,412	252,433	268,004	256,396	300,577
Fixed Assets	178,300	178,300	178,300	178,300	178,300
(Reserve for Depreciation)	(59,565)	(60,430)	(61,295)	(62,160)	(63,025)
Prepaid and Deferred Items	10,300	10,300	10,300	10,300	10,300
Other Assets	2,100	2,100	2,100	2,100	2,100
TOTAL ASSETS	361,547	382,703	397,409	384,936	428,252
Notes Payable—Bank and/or Fin. Co.	97,229	85,069	105,585	91,817	132,566
Current—Notes & Contracts	11,255	11,255	11,255	11,255	11,255
—Real Estate Mortgage	8,045	8,045	8,045	8,045	8,045
—2d Real Estate Mortgage	8,400	8,400	8,400	8,400	8,400
—New Equipment Loans	——	——	——	——	——
Accounts Payable	29,744	59,488	63,206	66,924	70,642
Accruals	12,400	12,400	12,400	12,400	12,400
Provision for Income Taxes	13,752	15,078	3,529	3,356	3,502
CURRENT LIABILITIES	180,825	199,735	212,420	202,197	246,810
Deferred—Notes & Contracts	26,084	25,168	24,252	23,336	22,419
—Real Estate Mortgage	45,584	45,168	44,752	44,336	43,919
—2d Real Estate Mortgage	16,600	16,200	15,800	15,400	15,000
—New Equipment Loans	——	——	——	——	——
Due to Officers	16,700	16,700	16,700	16,700	16,700
DEFERRED LIABILITIES	104,968	103,236	101,504	99,772	98,038
TOTAL LIABILITIES	285,793	302,971	313,924	301,969	344,848
Common Stock	10,000	10,000	10,000	10,000	10,000
Capital Surplus	10,000	10,000	10,000	10,000	10,000
Earned Surplus	55,754	59,732	63,485	62,967	63,404
NET WORTH	75,754	79,732	83,485	82,967	83,404
TOTAL, LIABILITIES & N. W.	361,547	382,703	397,409	384,936	428,252

Exhibit 84

INVENTORY—FINISHED GOODS; INVENTORY—RAW MATERIALS; INVENTORY—WORK IN PROCESS

All of these end-of-month figures were previously ascertained: see Exhibit 65.

FIXED ASSETS

The beginning balance for this account is changed by additions in July and November, as shown below:

SHEETS

JUNE	JULY	AUG.	SEPT.	OCT.	NOV.	DEC.
5,000	5,000	5,000	5,000	5,000	5,000	5,000
107,217	122,265	137,313	165,528	152,361	165,528	152,361
132,195	131,092	126,960	121,306	124,444	122,438	122,100
61,152	63,372	76,746	83,794	87,494	83,758	83,000
18,000	19,500	21,000	22,500	24,000	25,500	27,000
323,564	341,229	367,019	398,128	393,299	402,224	389,461
178,300	232,300	232,300	232,300	232,300	239,500	239,500
(63,890)	(65,205)	(66,520)	(67,835)	(69,150)	(70,525)	(71,900)
10,300	10,300	10,300	10,300	10,300	10,300	10,300
2,100	2,100	2,100	2,100	2,100	2,100	2,100
450,374	520,724	545,199	574,993	568,849	583,599	569,461
165,545	200,422	212,862	224,029	212,598	225,609	221,721
11,255	11,255	11,255	11,255	11,255	11,255	11,255
8,045	8,045	8,045	8,045	8,045	8,045	8,045
8,400	8,400	8,400	8,400	8,400	8,400	8,400
——	15,552	15,552	15,552	15,552	17,628	17,628
59,488	44,616	55,770	70,642	74,360	66,924	55,770
12,400	12,400	12,400	12,400	12,400	12,400	12,400
4,009	4,879	5,786	8,573	10,731	13,452	15,350
269,142	305,569	330,070	358,896	353,341	363,713	350,569
21,502	20,585	19,668	18,751	17,834	16,917	16,000
43,502	43,085	42,668	42,251	41,834	41,417	41,000
14,600	14,200	13,800	13,400	13,000	12,600	12,200
——	33,048	32,035	31,022	30,009	33,400	32,242
16,700	16,700	16,700	16,700	16,700	16,700	16,700
96,304	127,618	124,871	122,124	119,377	121,034	118,142
365,446	433,187	454,941	481,020	472,718	484,747	468,711
10,000	10,000	10,000	10,000	10,000	10,000	10,000
10,000	10,000	10,000	10,000	10,000	10,000	10,000
64,928	67,537	70,258	73,973	76,131	78,852	80,750
84,928	87,537	90,258	93,973	96,131	98,852	100,750
450,374	520,724	545,199	574,993	568,849	583,599	569,461

Exhibit 84 (cont'd)

Beginning balance	$178,300
July additions	54,000
	$232,300
November additions	7,200
	$239,500

Appropriate entries were made for the various months during the projection period.

RESERVE FOR DEPRECIATION

Calculations for this account were made, with reference to Exhibit 70, p. 100, as shown below:

Beginning balance	58,700	June balance	63,890
January	865	July	1,315
	59,565		65,205
February	865	August	1,315
	60,430		66,520
March	865	September	1,315
	61,295		67,835
April	865	October	1,315
	62,160		69,150
May	865	November	1,375
	63,025		70,525
June	865	December	1,375
	63,890		71,900

Beginning balance	58,700
Total for period (Ex. 70).	13,200
Total	71,900

PREPAID AND DEFERRED ITEMS

One type of account included under this caption is "Deferred Interest." To understand the nature of this asset, and how it is affected by the entries reflected in a projection, it may be well to go back and examine the origin of the account. Typically, deferred interest arises when equipment is purchased on a conditional sales contract, the amount of the interest representing the *total* of the interest that will be incurred *throughout* the period of the contract. For example, suppose that equipment with a cash price of $1,000.00 is purchased, with a 10 percent or $100.00 down payment being made and "add-on" interest of 6 percent being charged, payments to run for a period of 36 months. The "face" amount of the contract, then, would be $1,062.00, as shown below:

```
$1,000.00
 (100.00)
$ 900.00  Principal
   54.00  (6% of $900)
   54.00
   54.00
$1,062.00  (Principal plus 3 years'
                interest)
```

The monthly payment will be $29.50 ($1,062.00 divided by 36 months). The entries made at the outset would be as follows:

A.
	Debit			Credit	
Equipment	$1,000.00		Cash		$100.00
Deferred interest	162.00		Contract payable		1,062.00

Then, later, when a payment is made, the following entries would be made:

B.
	Debit			Credit	
Contract payable	$29.50		Cash		$29.50
Interest expense	$ 4.50		Deferred interest		$ 4.50

The $4.50 represents the amount of interest expense actually incurred for *one* month ($162.00 divided by 36 months).

In light of the above discussion, it should be clear that the *proper* way to handle *payments* on contracts already existing at the beginning of the projection period would be to "make entries" like those in "B," above. Actually, what was done was to provide enough cash for the *total* contract payment (see Exhibit 73, p. 104) and *also* enough cash for the interest; that is, cash disbursements were *exaggerated,* and the deferred interest related to the contracts was *not* reduced. Thus, the projection shows the *asset* "Prepaid and Deferred Items" as *more* than it should be, and the liability reflecting money needs, "Notes Payable—Bank and/or Finance Company" is also shown as *more* than it should be.

Similarly, when the new equipment was purchased (presumably on conditional sales contracts), entries such as those shown in "A," above, *should* have been reflected in the projection. Actually, however, what *was* done was to set up a liability representing the *principal* portion of the contract, only; no "deferred interest" asset was shown (see Exhibit 80).

Neither of the two "errors" pointed out above is sufficiently material to justify redoing the appropriate parts of the projection. They do, however, point out the necessity for "thinking straight" *and* in terms of entries, when projecting.

In view of the way contracts and payments on them were *actually* treated, the item "Prepaid and Deferred Items" remains unchanged throughout the projection period.

OTHER ASSETS

This account is assumed to undergo *no* changes during the projection period, so the beginning balance, from Exhibit 31, p. 40, was used throughout.

NOTES PAYABLE—BANK AND/OR FINANCE COMPANY

The amounts to be entered on the balance sheet for this item were calculated at the end of the last chapter; see line 6, Exhibit 83, from which the figures were posted to the balance sheet.

CURRENT—NOTES AND CONTRACTS

The current portion of these obligations, $11,255 (see Exhibit 35, p. 43, and Chapter 11), will not change during the period; payments are reflected in the *noncurrent* item (see below).

CURRENT—REAL ESTATE MORTGAGE

The current part of this obligation, $8,045 (see Chapter 11), will not change during the projection period. Reductions in the principal part of the debt will be reflected in the *deferred* part of the account (see below).

CURRENT—SECOND REAL ESTATE MORTGAGE

The current portion of this new item was calculated on the basis of total principal *and* interest payments amounting to approximately $700 per month, or $8,400 per year. (See Chapter 13.)

CURRENT—NEW EQUIPMENT LOANS

The current position of the two new equipment loans were calculated by multiplying the total monthly payment required (principal *and* interest), times 12 months ("current" is generally accepted to mean one year ahead); see Chapter 13 and the calculations below:

$1,296	$173	$15,552
×12	×12	2,076
$15,552	$2,076	$17,628

So, beginning when the first loan was obtained (July), $15,552 was shown as current; and the current portion of both loans—$17,628—was used for November and December, when both loans were outstanding.

ACCOUNTS PAYABLE

The assumptions made regarding accounts payable changed, it will be recalled, as various alternatives were considered (see Exhibit 80 and also Exhibit 83). The adjustments were made previously, but the *balance* of the account (with the *new* assumptions) as of the end of each month during the projection period has *not* previously been calculated. Therefore, it is necessary at this time to make such calculations; these are made in Exhibit 85.

ACCRUALS

Generally, in projecting, no attempt is made to allow for what are usually considered to be "minor" variations and fluctuations in this type of account. In this par-

ACCOUNTS PAYABLE

	JAN.	FEB.	MAR.	APR.	MAY	JUNE	JULY	AUG.	SEPT.	OCT.	NOV.	DEC.	TOTAL
1. Beg. Bal.	33,000[a]	29,744[g]	29,744	33,462	33,462	37,180	22,308	22,308	33,462	37,180	37,180	29,744	33,000[a]
2. Purchases[b]	29,744	29,744	33,462	33,462	37,180	22,308	22,308	33,462	37,180	37,180	29,744	26,026	371,800[b]
3. Subtotal	62,744	59,488	63,206	66,924	70,642	59,488	44,616	55,770	70,642	74,360	66,924	55,770	404,800
4. (Less Pay.)[c]	(33,000)[d]	(29,744)	(29,744)	(33,462)	(33,462)	(37,180)	(22,308)	(22,308)	(33,462)	(37,180)	(37,180)	(29,744)	(378,774)[e]
5. End. Bal.	29,744	29,744	33,462	33,462	37,180	22,308	22,308	33,462	37,180	37,180	29,744	26,026	26,026
6. "Advantage, Def. Basis"[f]		29,744	29,744	33,462	33,462	37,180	22,308	22,308	33,462	37,180	37,180	29,744	
7. Line 5 plus Line 6	29,744	59,488	63,206	66,924	70,642	59,488	44,616	55,770	70,642	74,360	66,924	55,770	
A. Beg. Bal.[a]	33,000[a]	29,744[g]	59,488	63,206	66,924	70,642	59,488	44,616	55,770	70,642	74,360	66,924	33,000[a]
B. Purchases[b]	29,744	29,744	33,462	33,462	37,180	22,308	22,308	33,462	37,180	37,180	29,744	26,026	371,800[b]
C. Subtotal	62,744	59,488	92,950	96,668	104,104	92,950	81,796	78,078	92,950	107,822	104,104	92,950	404,800
D. (Less Pay.)[h]	(33,000)	———	(29,744)	(29,744)	(33,462)	(33,462)	(37,180)	(22,308)	(22,308)	(33,462)	(37,180)	(37,180)	(349,030)[e]
E. End. Bal.	29,744	59,488	63,206	66,924	70,642	59,488	44,616	55,770	70,642	74,360	66,924	55,770	55,770

[a]From beg. balance sheet, Exhibit 1.
[b]From P & L, Exhibit 53.
[c]From Exhibit 72.
[d]From Line 10, Exhibit 73.
[e]Added "across."
[f]From Line 4, Exhibit 80.
[g]Ending balance Jan. col. is beg. bal. Feb. column, etc.
[h]Calculated on basis of paying 33,000 beg. bal. in Jan., and *thereafter* paying on a 60-day basis—i.e., *Jan.* purchases in *Mar.*, etc.

Exhibit 85

ticular instance, likewise, no adjustments were made, and the $12,400 shown on the last previous balance sheet (see Exhibit 31, p. 40) was used throughout the projection period.

PROVISION FOR INCOME TAXES

The beginning balance was taken from the last balance sheet (Exhibit 31); next, the accrual factor for January, February, and March was added (see Exhibit 66, p. 93, and the figures below), and then finally the March *payment* of the taxes was calculated. Thereafter, the cumulative provision as reflected in Exhibit 66 was used to complete the balance sheet.

Beginning balance	$12,800
January	952
	13,752
February	1,326
	15,078
March (prelim.)	1,251
	16,329
Less paym't	12,800
March (adj.)	$ 3,529

(April through December posted direct from Exhibit 66.)

DEFERRED—NOTES AND CONTRACTS

The monthly payments assumed on these debts (see Chapter 11 and also Exhibit 73, p. 104) were deducted from the deferred part of the item, as shown below:

Beginning balance	27,000	June balance	21,502
January	916	July	917
	26,084		20,585
February	916	August	917
	25,168		19,668
March	916	September	917
	24,252		18,751
April	916	October	917
	23,336		17,834
May	917	November	917
	22,419		16,917
June	917	December	917
	21,502		16,000

Beginning balance	27,000
Less principal payments	11,000
	16,000

DEFERRED—REAL ESTATE MORTGAGE

Again, starting with the *deferred* portion on the obligation, the *principal* portion of each monthly payment (see Chapter 12 and also Exhibit 73) was deducted to get the appropriate month-end balance:

Beginning balance	46,000	June balance	43,502
January	416	July	417
	45,584		43,085
February	416	August	417
	45,168		42,668
March	416	September	417
	44,752		42,251
April	416	October	417
	44,336		41,834
May	417	November	417
	43,919		41,417
June	417	December	417
	43,502		41,000

Beginning balance	46,000
Less principal payments	(5,000)
	41,000

DEFERRED—SECOND REAL ESTATE MORTGAGE

As with other debt, the monthly payments reduce what is shown as the *deferred* balance; see Chapter 13 and the calculations below:

Beginning balance	25,000	June balance	14,600
Current[a]	8,400	July	400
	16,600		14,200
February	400	August	400
	16,200		13,800
March	400	September	400
	15,800		13,400
April	400	October	400
	15,400		13,000
May	400	November	400
	15,000		12,600
June	400	December	400
	14,600		12,200

[a]417 plus 292 interest first month; current portion estimated at 700 per month (700x12 equals 8,400)

Current	8,400
Deferred	12,200
End balance	20,600
Payments	4,400 (11 × 400 principal payments)
Beginning balance	25,000

DEFERRED—NEW EQUIPMENT LOANS

To make sure that the calculations were made correctly, payments on these obligations (see Chapter 13) were deducted separately for each of the two loans, and then their *combined* balance calculated:

Loan No. 1

Beginning balance	48,600
Current[a]	15,552
Deferred balance	33,048
August	1,013[b]
	32,035
September	1,013
	31,022
October	1,013
	30,009
November	1,013
	28,996
December	1,013
End balance—def.	27,983

[a]1296 total payment per month times 12 equals 15,552, current portion.
[b]Principal portion of payment.

Beginning balance	48,600
	5,065 (5 × 1,013)
End balance	43,535
Current	15,552
Deferred	27,983

Loan No. 2

Beginning balance	6,480
Current[a]	2,076
Deferred balance	4,404
Deferred	145[b]
End balance	4,259

[a]173 total payment per month times 12 equals 2,076, current portion.
[b]Principal portion of payment.

Beginning balance	6,480
	145
End balance	6,335
Current	2,076
Deferred	4,259

DEFERRED PORTION—NEW EQUIPMENT LOANS

July		*November*	
33,048		28,996	
August		4,404	
32,035		33,400	
September		*December*	
31,022		27,983	
October		4,259	
30,009		32,242	

DUE TO OFFICERS; COMMON STOCK; CAPITAL SURPLUS

No change was contemplated for these accounts, so the balances as shown in the last balance sheet (Exhibit 31) were used throughout the projection period.

EARNED SURPLUS

The monthly profits and losses, as reflected on the completed P. & L. (Exhibit 65, p. 90), were applied to the beginning balance, as shown below, to get the appropriate figure for each monthly balance sheet:

Beginning balance	52,900	June balance	64,928
January	2,854	July	2,609
	55,754		67,537
February	3,978	August	2,721
	59,732		70,258
March	3,753	September	3,715
	63,485		73,973
April	(518)	October	2,158
	62,967		76,131
May	437	November	2,721
	63,404		78,852
June	1,524	December	1,898
	64,928		80,750

Beginning balance	52,900
Profits for year	27,850
	80,750

"TOTALING"

Now—at long last—the projection process is completed! That is, *if* the balance sheets we so painstakingly built up *do balance.* . . .

The pains taken to "prove out" each step in the projection process turned out to be worthwhile: totals were added up, and the assets *do* equal the liabilities and net worth—no small achievement, since we have given effect to, literally, several hundred separate "entries."

Next, attention turns to, "What do we *do* with all this?"

WHAT IF YOU DON'T BALANCE?

If, by chance, your balance sheets do *not* balance, when you get to the appropriate point, don't be concerned: it is always relatively easy to track down the error or errors. The first thing you do is to go ahead and get *a* total asset figure, and *a* total liability and net worth figure, for each month end. Next you figure out the *difference* between the two totals, if any, for *each* month end. Then you *study* the pattern: are you off the *same* figure each month—or for some of the dates? Does the amount of the variance "build" from one month end to the next? Etc.

By "backtracking" each item to its "source" working paper you will gradually find each and every error—and as you keep adjusting your "variance" totals as you find mistakes, you will gradually "zero" out the differences—and become balanced.

Now, on to the *uses* that we can make of this projection.

15

How to Use
the Projection

A well-designed budget program is an effective management mechanism for forecasting realizable results over a definite period or periods, for planning and coordinating the various operations and functions of the business to achieve realizable results, and for so controlling and limiting any variations from the approved plan of action that the desired results are realized.

> —Page 10, Section 4,
> *Accountants' Handbook,* 4th ed.,
> Ronald Press, 1965
> (emphasis supplied)

IN THINKING ABOUT HOW TO USE ALL THE MATERIAL AND INFORMATION developed in the course of this projection effort, management found it helpful to think, first, in terms of two *types* of use: "internal" and "external."

One of the prime purposes of the projection is *external*—namely, to help convince lenders to provide the money needed to carry out the program. This aspect of using the projection will be treated separately in the next chapter.

Internally, with respect to the description of a budget program appearing at the head of this chapter, the projection has already achieved the first objective ("forecasting results"). What is left to consider, then, are the other two objectives: "planning and coordinating operations" and "controlling and limiting variations."

In casting about for ways and means of making sure that all of the work done so far in the projection would not be lost, but instead would be woven into the daily patterns of activity in the business—so as to achieve the maximum benefits of an effective budget program—management found itself looking back over the projection, chapter by chapter, and making notes.

MANAGEMENT'S PRINCIPAL GOALS

By reviewing its notes, management soon concluded that *one* way of proceeding would be to summarize its own principal goals; that is, to list in an orderly fashion those points which it intends to follow up on with the most vigor—those items which reflect management's principal concerns, on reviewing the whole projection.

Using such a process, it found that it was weighing "two sides" of a question: could it overcome the fact that the projection indicated more extensive borrowing than originally anticipated, with accompanying interest costs that could seriously undermine the projected profits; and if so, *how?*

Gradually, thinking along this route, management drew up this chart:

"Problem"	"Solutions?"
1. Total projected interest cost.	1. Reduce maximum interest cost by getting bank to participate 50% in the receivable-inventory loan.
2. (*Less* what *is* provided for in the projection).	
3. *Equals* net "extra interest" costs—to be overcome, in some fashion.	2. So adjust borrowings that the monthly *average* loan will be *less* than reflected in the end-of-month projected figures.
	3. Collect accounts receivable faster, reduce 57 days to 45 days.
	4. Do *not* spend "unallocated" manufacturing expenses.
	5. Do *not* spend "other charges."
	6. Improve gross profit %.
	7. Eliminate planned salary increase for president.
	8. Defer hiring of controller.

Next, it seemed logical to put a "price tag" on the "problem," and on the "solutions." First, it was necessary to focus on the receivable-inventory loan, since it represents the maximum stress in the borrowing picture. These figures were reviewed (see Exhibit 86) and the key figure emerging from the analysis was the *average* loan figure—$164,588.

Next, the *total* interest costs were reviewed (see Exhibit 87). It was determined that the "worst possible" situation would be if the bank refused to participate at all in the loan, and all borrowings were at the finance company rate. In that event, total borrowing costs would amount to $35,919, or $17,919 *more* than the $18,000 projected. *That* is the problem. . . .

Turning to the other side of the coin, the first "solution" would be to persuade

FINANCE COMPANY AND/OR BANK BORROWING

	ESTIMATED END OF MONTH BALANCE[a]
January	$ 97,229
February	85,069
March	105,585
April	91,817
May	132,566
June	165,545
July	200,422
August	212,862
September	224,029
October	212,598
November	225,609
December	221,721
TOTAL	$1,975,052
AVERAGE[b]	$ 164,588

[a]From line 6, Exhibit 83.
[b]Total divided by twelve.

Exhibit 86

SUMMARY—INTEREST ASSUMPTIONS

	AVERAGE	RATE	INTEREST
Real Estate Mortgage	$43,500	7%	$ 3,045
Existing Notes & Contracts	a	Various	3,255
Second Mortgage, Factory Building	22,500	14%	3,150
Borrowing on New Equip.—"Loan 1"	b	7% "Add-on"	1,701
Borrowing on New Equip.—"Loan 2"	c	7% "Add-on"	76
Finance Company/Bank Loan	164,588[d]	12%[e]	19,751[f]
TOTAL			$30,978[g]

[a]See Chapter 11.
[b]Six months at $283.50 per month equals $1,701; see Chapter 13.
[c]Two months at $37.80 per month equals $76; Chapter 13.
[d]See Exhibit 86.
[e]Assumes that bank participation to the extent of 50% obtained, that bank rate is 8%, that finance company rate is 15%, and that finance company is paid 1% service fee on bank's 50% (8 plus 1 equals 9, plus 15 equals 24, divided by two gives average of 12).
[f]If the bank should decide *not* to participate at all in the loan, the finance company rate—assumed to be 15%—would apply to the *entire* loan, and interest costs would increase $4,941, to $24,692.
[g]If all of receivable-inventory loan was at 15% (see [f] above), total interest costs would increase $4,941 to $35,919.

Exhibit 87

the bank to participate to the extent of 50 percent in the receivable-inventory loan. This would save an estimated $4,941 (see footnote[f], Exhibit 87).

Second, management had been particularly interested in one point made early in its discussion with the commercial finance company. Specifically, that company's executive had stressed that in working with them, with all of the cash flowing through the finance company, that companies often borrowed *much less* ("20 to 35 percent less") than they otherwise might, when borrowing on a note from the bank. That is, the loan would "peak out" when payables were paid, then drop as daily receivable collections were turned over to the finance company and applied to the loan balance, rising somewhat for payroll needs, etc., but then dropping again. In guessing at the "price tag" on this "solution" management estimated that *average daily borrowings* (the figure on which interest would be calculated), would run 20 percent *less* than indicated by the projected month-end figures. This would result in savings of $3,950 (20 percent of $19,751, the total interest on the receivable-inventory loan, assuming bank participation at 50 percent; see Exhibit 87).

The third "solution"—collecting receivables faster than the "57 days'" basis used in the projection—is an inviting possibility. But, realistically, management recognizes that it may take some time to change existing collection or payment patterns. So it assumed *no* improvement during the first six months of the projection period, but that the days' index would drop to *45* days' during the second half of the year, representing a *20 percent* improvement. Applied to indicated borrowing for the second half of the year (Exhibit 86), the 20 percent means that on an average $42,000 *less* would be borrowed, which would result in saving approximately $2,500 during this period ($42,000 times 12 percent divided by 2).

In estimated manufacturing expenses, to be conservative, a $6,200 "unallocated" item was included (see Chapter 10). In other words, management can "save" that amount by simply making sure that a figure *not* representing any specific, known needs is *not used*. . . .

Similarly, when "Other Charges" were considered, no one could think of anything that would occur resulting in such an item of cost or expense, but *$3,000* was allocated, anyway. So, if management can *keep* this figure at "zero" it will save $3,000.

When the implications of cash flow were being considered, management indicated that while it did *not* wish to "count on it" in preparing the projection, it *was* confident that at least *2 percent* more gross profit could be obtained, over and above the 21.2 percent projected, pointing out that the resulting *23.2 percent* would still be *less* than the *23.6 percent* achieved last year. Management believes that by a combination of selective price increases and reduction in costs, and an improvement in inventory turn, it can *easily* make up the 2 percent—which would yield a "saving" of $16,200. (See Chapter 13.)

Next, if projected results are *not* being met, management plans on foregoing a projected raise of $4,800 a year effective beginning in August. This would result in a "savings" of $1,800 during the year (see Chapter 11).

Finally, management now feels that, if it must, it can continue to get along without the controller programed to join the staff in August at $1,000 a month. This step, if it becomes necessary, would "save" $5,000 during the projection period (see Chapter 11).

Recapitulating, here is how management's alternatives "weighed in:"

Max. interest	$35,919	1. Get bank partic.	$ 4,941
Less projected	18,000	2. Borrow less	3,950
Problem	$17,919	3. Collect rec. faster	2,500
		4. Save "Unalloc." mfg. exp.	6,200
		5. Save "O/C"	3,000
		6. Improve G.P.%	16,200
		7. Do *not* raise pr. sal.	1,800
		8. Do *not* hire controller	5,000
			$43,591

All in all, management feels that, by focusing attention on these particular parts of the projected program, it can be confident that it will at *least* achieve the projected profit objectives. . . .

COORDINATING AND CONTROLLING

As it gave further consideration to the problems involved (now that the projection was finished) in *coordinating* all of the various parts of the program, and in *controlling* the activities that "lay behind" each of the figures in the projection, management came to realize that much *groundwork* had already been laid. By the *process* of having key employees *participate* in the projection process, each participant has had an opportunity to see how their particular "bailiwick" fits into the overall picture. Also, each participant can now sense the need to *monitor* his or her performance, if the overall objectives are to be achieved.

The need, then, became a little clearer: to "break down" the projection into "pieces," giving certain *portions* of it to *individuals* within the organization.

Thinking along these lines, and recognizing the need to "marry smoothly" any *new* procedures and practices with these *existing* ones, management also was reminded that it "wears several hats" itself. That is, it functions one moment as Sales Manager, another as Credit Manager, etc. So one *primary* need is for management *itself* to get so organized that it is "wearing its hats" in the right style, at the right time, effectively.

Ultimately—and somewhat experimentally—management began to organize its thinking in terms of *days of the week* ("after all, most of these figures have to be watched on a weekly or daily basis, so I'd better use my *present* 'modus operandi' as a base, and plan how I intend to use my *own* time each week").

Monday

Traditionally, management has started off the week with a sales meeting. This has been effective, and will be continued. To make the meeting more effective, however, three reports will be prepared in advance of the meeting:

Sales Report
Backlog Report
Sales Expense Report

Each of these reports (see Exhibit 88, Exhibit 89, and Exhibit 90) is designed to keep management posted on progress with respect to sales-related activities reflected in the projection. The Office Manager will be responsible for having these reports ready by Monday morning.

In addition, management intends to review the advertising program each Monday, as well as reflect on the status of prices and the possibilities of obtaining increases in them.

Tuesday

Tuesday was arbitrarily designated as the day on which to pay particular attention to accounts receivable.

The old accounts receivable aging report was modified (see Exhibit 91), and

---

SALES REPORT

Date ....

As of ....

	LAST MONTH		LAST WEEK		YEAR-TO-DATE	
	EST.	ACTUAL	EST.[a]	ACTUAL	EST.[a]	ACTUAL
I. UNIT SALES						
Product A						
B						
C						
D						
E						
TOTAL						
II. PRODUCTS—$						
Product A						
B						
C						
D						
E						
Service						
Misc.						
TOTAL						
III. SALESMAN—$						
"S"						
"J"						
"New"						
"House"						
Agents						
Misc.						
TOTAL						

Submitted by ....

---

[a]Pro-rate by working days per month.

Exhibit 88

BACKLOG REPORT

Date ....

As of ....

UNSHIPPED ORDERS
IN PROCESS

I. NUMBER OF UNITS:
    Product A
            B
            C
            D
            E
    TOTAL

II. DOLLAR VALUE OF ORDERS (Approximate):
    Product A $
            B
            C
            D
            E
    TOTAL $

Submitted by ....

Exhibit 89

SALES EXPENSE REPORT

Date ....

As of ....

YEAR-TO-DATE
(THRU LAST MONTH-END)

	ESTIMATED	ACTUAL	EST., THIS MONTH	"JOURNAL TOTAL"[a]
Salaries & Commissions				
Travel & Entertainment				
Advertising				
Delivery Expense				
Depreciation				
TOTAL				

Submitted by ....

[a]Derived from analysis of journal entries made so far during the month.

Exhibit 90

ACCOUNTS RECEIVABLE AGING

Date ....
As of ....

CUSTOMER, ADDRESS	NAME OF CONTACT, TEL. NUMBER	TOTAL OWING	0–30 DAYS	30–60 DAYS	60–90 DAYS	90–120 DAYS	OLDER	COMMENT

NOTE: As the *last page* of each aging, show the following information:
1. Last month's Net Sales $ _____
2. Last month's Net Sales divided by 30 equals $ _____ (*one* days' Sales).
3. Total balance on this date, Accounts Receivable $ _____
4. Item "3" above divided by Item "2" equals _____ "Days' Sales in A/C Rec."
5. 57 Days' projected; Item "4" above _____ Days Less (or More!)
6. Advantage (or DIS-Advantage) $ _____ (Item "5" times Item "2").

Exhibit 91

was to be completed by no later than the eleventh of each month. The office secretary was to be responsible for preparing this report, and for marking payments received on the report, so it is updated each Monday to show the present status of accounts, and given to management early each Tuesday. One prime management goal as to receivables is to "beat" the predicted result of having 10 percent of accounts eliminated as a borrowing base because they are too old.

As part of keeping a "feel" toward receivables, management also plans to continue reviewing the monthly statements of account prepared shortly after the end of each month, prior to their being sent out. They should be ready by the third of each month.

Around the twentieth of each month management has made it a practice to "take a second look" at receivables, with an eye to seeing what phone calls should be made, etc., to bring in as much money as possible before the end of the month. A report for this function has been drafted (see Exhibit 92), and the office secretary—who will be groomed more than in the past to serve as a Credit Manager in addition to her other duties—will be responsible for preparing this report by the twenty-third of each month. Eventually management wants to establish *credit limits* for each account, and to show them on the aging report and the report of the twenty-third.

RECEIVABLES COLLECTION REPORT

Date ....

As of ....

(Submit *with* updated aging report)

A. Sales Last Month ....$

B. Collections so far this month ....$

C. Accounts which have made, and *not kept* promises; consider ready for "Special Attention" and follow-up by Salesman or President:

D. Accounts which are, herewith, nominated to receive a collection letter (indicate Letter A, Letter B, Letter C, or specially written letter):

E. Accounts where "all previous efforts" have failed, and which are ready to be turned over to a collection agency and/or an attorney:

Submitted by ....

Exhibit 92

Again on an arbitrary basis, management selected Tuesday as the time to review general and administrative expenses. Working with the Bookkeeper, it shouldn't be too much trouble for the Office Manager to have a suitable report (see Exhibit 93) ready each Tuesday morning. Note also that this report includes information on "other charges," where management sees a potential $3,000 saving.

GENERAL AND ADMINISTRATIVE EXPENSE REPORT[a]

Date ....

As of ....

	YEAR-TO-DATE (THRU LAST MONTH-END)			
	ESTIMATED	ACTUAL	EST., THIS MONTH	"JOURNAL TOTAL"[b]
Executive Salaries				
Office Salaries				
Office Suppl. & Sta.				
Postage				
Telephone				
Professional Services				
Insurance—General				
Insurance—Empl. Hos.				
Payroll Taxes				
Personal Property Taxes				
Real Estate Taxes				
Bad Debts				
Collection Expense				
Dues & Subscriptions				
Bank Charges				
Depreciation				
Interest				
Utilities				
Repairs & Mtce.				
Misc.				
TOTAL				
Other Charges—In Detail:				

Submitted by ....

[a]Also O/C
[b]Derived from analysis of journal entries made so far during the month.

Exhibit 93

Finally, management decided to devote a portion of each Tuesday to "personnel matters." Wearing its "Personnel Manager hat" on Tuesdays, management plans to then consider the vital matters of hiring, firing, raises, etc. To make sure that it follows up on all of the many decisions of this type that have been incorporated in the projection, management reviewed the entire projection again—strictly from a personnel vantage point—and came up with a "management personnel list" (see Exhibit 94). This list will be reviewed and updated each Tuesday.

"MANAGEMENT PERSONNEL LIST"

A. Hiring of new factory employees.

B. Hiring of new salesman, January.

C. Hiring of new indirect labor—$6,000 man, January.

D. Hiring of new supervisor—$4,800 man, July.

E. Hiring of new controller—$12,000 year, August.

F. Hiring of new indirect labor clerk—$3,265, August.

G. Work closely with *new* men, check up on their orientation progress:
     1. $7,200 man just hired, supervisory.
     2. New salesman.
     3. New indirect labor—$6,000 man.
     (etc.)

H. Review entire staff with respect to raises and promotions, and follow up on raises included in projection:
     1. January increase of $1,500—supervisor.
     2. January increase of $500—supervisor.
     3. January increase of $500 for $5,500 man, indirect labor.
     4. January increase of $300 for $4,000 man, indirect labor.
     5. August, President, $4,800 year.
     6. September, $200 month for raises, supervisory staff.

I. ???Develop secretary into Credit Manager?

J. ???Develop Office Manager into Controller?

K. Develop information of Profit Sharing Program.

Exhibit 94

Wednesday

In the past, one problem management has had has been keeping current as to accounts payable information. This problem has been due in part to the fact that all bills don't come in until about the thirteenth of the month, so a current accounts payable aging is not available until after then—although it is necessary to make at least some payments (where discounts are involved) before the tenth.

In future, because payable policies play such an important part in management's financing plans, more attention must be devoted to this subject. To assure this, a new accounts payable aging format has been prepared (see Exhibit 95). It will be noted that this report calls for "coding" each account as to how it should normally be paid. The background information for the "coding" has already been developed. This report is to be prepared by the Bookkeeper—who pays the bills—by no later than the sixteenth of each month.

And, to solve the "old" problem, a *new* report will be prepared by the book-keeper by the seventh of each month, detailing *proposed* payments on payables (see Exhibit 96).

Wednesday was also selected as the time to review the status of the finished goods inventory. A suitable report form was drafted (see Exhibit 97). This report should be prepared by the Shipping Clerk each Tuesday afternoon (insofar as the *physical count* is concerned), and finished up by the Office Manager so as to be ready for management on Wednesday morning. This area is one of the most promising, if inventory turn is to be improved upon.

ACCOUNTS PAYABLE AGING

Date ....
As of ....

VENDOR	SUPPLIER OF	PAY'MT CODE[a]	TERMS	TOTAL OWING	0–30 DAYS	30–60 DAYS	60–90 DAYS	90–120 DAYS	OLDER	COMMENT

"Trade Payables":

"Expense Payables":

[a]Code either "10" "30" "60" "90" (days), or *Special*.

Exhibit 95

150

PROPOSED PAYMENTS ON PAYABLES

(Submit *with* updated aging report,   Date ....
and list *in order* in which vendors
appear on aging.)   As of ....

| | AMOUNT OF | |
| VENDOR | PROPOSED PAYMENT | COMMENT |

Submitted by ....

Exhibit 96

In addition, *some* time must be set aside for new products each week; those new to the line, those in an earlier stage of development, and those still to be developed all make this an important "hat" for management to wear, and it designated Wednesday as that day. . . .

Thursday

Because production is such a vital function, and as yet unconsidered, Thursday became "production day." First to be considered was the status of finished goods production, for which a suitable report form was drafted (see Exhibit 98). Next was the matter of labor (see Exhibit 99). Raw material and WIP inventories have to be watched, if they are to turn faster, and Exhibit 100 was designed to develop required information. Finally, manufacturing expenses were to be reviewed on Thursdays, the review being based on a report (see Exhibit 101).

FINISHED GOODS INVENTORY REPORT

Date ....

	LAST MONTH	NEXT MONTH
Estimated End-of-Month Balance	$	$
Actual Balance Today (see below)*		$...........................

PRODUCT	I NUMBER OF UNITS ON HAND	II ESTIMATED COST PER UNIT	III COL. I × COL. II	IV NUMBER OF UNITS SOLD LAST MONTH
A	....	$.......................	$.......................	....
B	....	....	....	....
C	....	....	....	....
D	....	....	....	....
E	....	....	....	....
TOTAL			$...........................*	

Submitted by ....

Exhibit 97

PRODUCTION REPORT

Date ....

As of ....

PRODUCT	YEAR-TO-DATE		LAST MONTH		LAST WEEK		NEXT WEEK?
	ESTIM.	ACTUAL	ESTIM.	ACTUAL	ESTIM.[a]	ACTUAL	ESTIMATED[a]
A							
B							
C							
D							
E							
TOTAL							

Submitted by ....

[a]Pro-rate on basis of number of working days in month.

Exhibit 98

LABOR REPORT

Date ....

As of ....

| | $ OF LABOR | | PERCENTAGE VARIANCE— |
	ESTIMATED	ACTUAL	PLUS OR (MINUS)
Year-to-Date			
Last Month			
Last Week[a]			
Next Week[a]			

Submitted by ....

---

[a]Pro-rate on basis of number of working days per month.

Exhibit 99

Being related to production, the matter of *equipment* also deserves special attention, and management plans to wear this "hat" also on Thursday. In particular, management noted several specific items it wants to review carefully at least once a week:

1. $1,000 a month for January, February, and March repairs and maintenance.
2. $2,000 a month, March and April, engineering expenses.
3. $54,000 of new equipment, July. (It *may* prove feasible to get this in earlier —and to get a larger gross profit % as a result. . . .)
4. $7,200 of new equipment, November. Earlier?

Friday

Borrowing is to be reviewed each Friday morning, when the Office Manager, who is to be responsible for this report, gives it to management (see Exhibit 102). The goal here is to "maximize" borrowing *power* (availability) and "minimize" actual borrowings.

Financial statements for the previous month are to be ready by the twenty-first of each month, and—after review—copies are to be forwarded to the lenders requiring them. In order to make them more useful, management has instructed the bookkeeper and Office Manager (both of whom work on the statements) that there are to be three columns for each figure: Actual, Estimated, and "Variance."

Assuming the bank agrees to participate with the finance company, management plans on meeting each month: first, with the finance company (about the twenty-fifth) and then with the bank (about the thirtieth).

Quality control is another point requiring periodic special attention from management. A report designed to assure such review each Friday was prepared (see Exhibit 103). The balance of Friday management intends to allocate for "troubleshooting" —for whatever area seems to be most in need of attention.

RAW MATERIALS AND *WIP* INVENTORY REPORT

Date ....

As of ....

	YEAR-TO-DATE	
I. RAW MATERIALS INVENTORY POSITION	ESTIMATED	ACTUAL

Beginning Inventory
Plus Purchases
Less "Materials Est. in Fin. Gds. Inventory"
Less "Materials Est. in Sales"
Equals Est. *Present* Inventory

II. WIP INVENTORY POSITION
    A. Estimated—End of *Last* Month $
    B. Estimated—End of *Next* Month $
    C. Actual this date (see below) $

	STATE OF COMPLETION	NO. OF UNITS	COST VALUE—$	COL. 2 × COL. 3—$
Product A	25%			
	50%			
	75%			
B	25%			
	50%			
	75%			
C	25%			
	50%			
	75%			
D	25%			
	50%			
	75%			
E	25%			
	50%			
	75%			
TOTAL				$............................

Submitted by ....

Exhibit 100

MANUFACTURING EXPENSE REPORT

Date ....

As of ....

| | YEAR-TO-DATE (THRU LAST MONTH END) | | EST., THIS MONTH | "JOURNAL TOTAL"[a] |
	ESTIMATED	ACTUAL		
Supervis. Salaries				
Indirect Labor				
Depreciation				
Repairs & Mtce.				
Supplies				
Payroll Taxes				
Engineering Exp.				
Misc.				
"Unallocated"				
TOTAL				

Submitted by ....

[a]Derived from analysis of journal entries made so far during the month.

Exhibit 101

Management is used to working Saturdays and sometimes Sundays, but *doesn't* want to plan on that basis, except for allotting one Saturday late in the month for "reprojecting" one month ahead.

CALENDARS

To summarize its plans as they were developed, management found it convenient to prepare two calendars:

Weekly Calendar (Exhibit 104).
Monthly Calendar (Exhibit 105).

The timing of functions for the President *and* for the Office Manager are shown on both calendars. In the absence of a Controller, the Office Manager will, by following up on various reports, serve to do some controlling himself, and make it easier for the President to "wear the Controller's hat."

As "fallout" from its note-taking and calendar-making, management came up with a tentative list of office functions, which it gave to the Office Manager as an embryonic "job description" (see Exhibit 106).

Feeling well organized for future action, management next turned its attention to the key problem facing it: to arrange to *finance* its program.

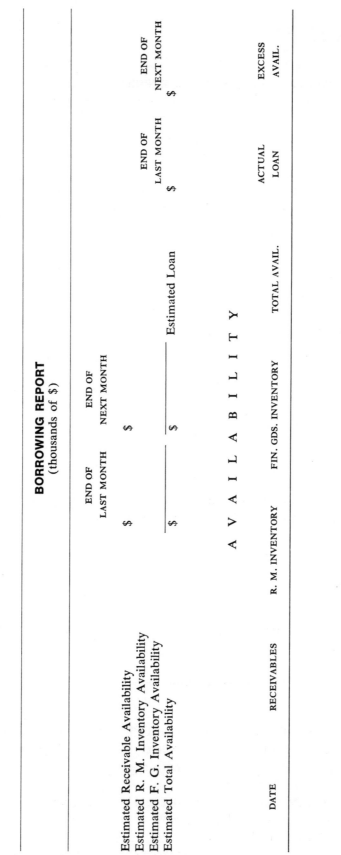

BORROWING REPORT
(thousands of $)

	END OF LAST MONTH	END OF NEXT MONTH
Estimated Receivable Availability		
Estimated R. M. Inventory Availability		
Estimated F. G. Inventory Availability	$	$
Estimated Total Availability	$	$

Estimated Loan

A V A I L A B I L I T Y

DATE	RECEIVABLES	R. M. INVENTORY	FIN. GDS. INVENTORY	TOTAL AVAIL.	END OF LAST MONTH $	ACTUAL LOAN	END OF NEXT MONTH $	EXCESS AVAIL.

Exhibit 102

QUALITY CONTROL REPORT

Date ....

As of ....

A. Scrap Sales—Year to Date $

B. Complaints Received This Week (Letters, Calls, etc.—Attach Copies):

C. Warranty Claims Made This Week (Describe Nature of Problem, Date of Production Indicated by Serial No.):

D. Number of Units Returned from Final Assembly for Rework:

(Classify by Nature of Defect)

PRODUCT
   A
   B
   C
   D
   E
    TOTAL

E. *Returns and Allowances—$:*

	ESTIMATED	ACTUAL

YEAR-TO-DATE:
   $
   % to Gross Sales

LAST MONTH:
   $
   % to Gross Sales

F. Inspector's Summary (*Including* Suggestions for Decreasing Defects):

Submitted by ....

Exhibit 103

WEEKLY CALENDAR

	SUNDAY	MONDAY	TUESDAY	WEDNESDAY	THURSDAY	FRIDAY	SATURDAY
For the President:		Sales meeting Review backlog Review adv. prog. Review sell. exp.	Review receivables Review G. & A. exp. "Wear personnel hat."	Review payables Review F. G. Inv. "New product day"	Review produc. Review labor Rev. R. M. WIP inv. Rev. mfg. exp. "Equip. day."	Rev. borrow. Rev. qual. control. "Trbleshtg."	
For the Office:		Update rec. aging Update G. & A. exp. rpt.	Update pay. aging Update fin. gds. inv. records	Update produc. rpt. Update labor rpt. Update R. M. WIP inv. rpt. Update mfg. exp. rpt.	Update bor. rpt. Update qual. ctrl. rpt.	Update sales rpts. Update backlog rpt. Update sell. exp. rpt.	

Exhibit 104

MONTHLY CALENDAR

	(PRESIDENT)	(OFFICE)
1		
2		
3	Review customers' statements	Statements out to customers
4		
5		
6		Prepare draft, proposed payments on payables
7	Review proposed payments on payables	
8		
9		
10		Complete accounts receivable aging
11	Review new accounts receivable aging	
12		
13		
14		
15		Complete accounts payable aging
16	Review new accounts payable aging	Prepare trial balance
17		
18		
19		
20		Complete financial statements
21	Review new financial statements	
22	Forward copies of fin. sts. to lenders	Prepare receivable collection report
23	Review receivable collection report	
24		
25	Meet with finance company	
26		
27		
28	"Reproject" one month ahead	
29		
30	Meet with bank	

Exhibit 105

OFFICE FUNCTIONS[a]

1. Review factory time cards.
2. Prepare payrolls.
3. Prepare, maintain vacation schedules.
4. Pay accounts payable.
5. Collect accounts receivable.
6. Maintain borrowing records.
7. Make loan payments.
8. Submit payroll tax reports, payments.
9. Prepare monthly "tickler," insurance, other reports.
10. Forward reports to lenders.
11. Post journals, ledgers.
12. Handle dictation, correspondence.
13. Filing.

[a]In *addition* to functions listed on "Monthly Calendar," Exhibit 105.

Exhibit 106

16

The Five C's of Credit

Credit really boils down to man's confidence in man.

—Old credit saying

THE ACTION BEGINS

FOR SOME TIME THE EMPHASIS HAS BEEN ON PLANNING, AND ESTIMATing. Now the time has come for some action. . . .

First, management contacted the head of a company making second mortgages, and made arrangements for their people to come out and make an appraisal or whatever they needed to do to reach a decision concerning a request for a $25,000, five-year second mortgage. Second, management called the commercial finance company executive it had visited previously, and made arrangements for him to come out the following Monday morning. Finally, management called the bank vice-president with whom it was accustomed to work, and made an appointment to see him the following Friday morning at the bank. (The idea is to *first* confront the banker with the program on his own ground, to get him interested, and *then* invite him out to take a good look around the factory.)

SECOND THOUGHTS

Next management paused to reflect a little about what it would try to accomplish during the bank visit and just how it wanted to approach the matter of the bank participating in a loan made by a finance company. It even considered the possibility of pretending *not* to believe that the projected receivable-inventory loan—as outlined in pro-forma balance sheets—was not "bankable" ("after all, I *won't know* that, for sure, until the bank says no"). In the end, however, it was decided that it might be poor psychology to have the bank say no, and that it would make it clear early in the discussion that it seriously doubted that the bank could go along 100 percent —*but* that it certainly hoped the bank *would* be able to participate in a finance company loan to the extent of 50 percent. *If* it seemed appropriate, at *some* point in the discussion management decided it *might* restate that, and say it hoped "*a bank*" would be able to participate (management *has* been approached by other banks, over the years. . . .).

Recalling the last visit it had with the banker, management remembered the emphasis: "After all, we have to know when our loan will be repaid—and your needs have simply been going in one direction, *up.*" And, it also recalled a fundamental point, about there being only *three* ways to pay back money: from the sale of assets, from profits or other additions to net worth (such as from the sale of stock), and by borrowing from one lender to repay another. Which led to the question, "What answer do I have, when the banker asks about how we can pay back *this* loan?"

Musing over these ideas, management decided to refresh its memory regarding cash flow—to see how *much* debt it *could* repay, looking ahead. In taking this fresh look, it decided to include *interest* as part of cash flow: part of its present and part of its future debt was in the form of conditional sales contracts, and what was shown as "current" (due within a year) on those obligations included principal *and* interest; so it seemed logical to count in interest when considering "debt service" (see exhibit 107). The key fact: projected cash flow (profit and depreciation) of $41,050— $59,050 if you add in interest. What has to be *paid* with this cash flow? Again, the

PROJECTED CASH FLOW

YEAR	I PROFIT[a]	II DEPRECIA- TION	III "CASH FLOW"[b]	IV INTEREST	V "GROSS CASH FLOW"[c]
1	$ 6,000	$ 3,200	$ 9,200	$ 400	$ 9,600
2	12,700	3,500	16,200	1,800	18,000
3	(200)	4,700	4,500	4,800	9,300
4	6,600	8,500	15,100	8,300	23,400
5	23,800	9,000	32,800	12,000	44,800
?Next Year	27,850[d]	13,200[e]	41,050	18,000[f]	59,050

[a]For past years, see Exhibit 30.
[b]Col. I plus Col. II.
[c]Col. III plus Col. IV.
[d]See Exhibit 65.
[e]See Exhibit 73.
[f]See Exhibit 64.

Exhibit 107

appropriate figures were assembled (see Exhibit 108). Key fact: for the projection period ahead, there was $34,106 of serial debt to be met, so there was a 20 percent margin, even if you *don't* count interest as cash flow:

	41,050	Available (*Just* Profit and Deprec.)
100%	34,106	Needed
20%	6,944	

Looking at it *another* way, there were $23,200 of *principal* payments to be met (See Exhibit 108) and there should have been $27,850 of profit to handle them. Then, you could say there was depreciation and interest of $31,200 ($13,200 plus $18,000) to meet the interest requirements on the *serial* debt ($10,906, Exhibit 108), *plus* providing interest for the receivable-inventory loan. And, the amount left for the receivable-inventory loan, $20,294 ($31,200 less $10,906), would support an average loan of $169,000 at 12 percent ($20,294 divided by 12)—versus a projected average receivable-inventory loan of $164,588 (Exhibit 86).

SERIAL DEBT REQUIREMENTS

YEAR AHEAD:	PRINCIPAL	INTEREST	TOTAL
1. 1st R. E. Mtge.	$ 5,000[a]	$ 3,045[b]	$ 8,045
2. 2d R. E. Mtge.	5,000[c]	3,150[b]	8,150
3. Existing notes and contrs.	8,000[a]	3,255[b]	11,255[a]
4. New Equip. Loan No. 1	5,065[c]	1,418[c]	6,483
5. New Equip. Loan No. 2	135[c]	38[c]	173
TOTAL	$23,200	$10,906	$34,106

SECOND YEAR:	PRINCIPAL	INTEREST	TOTAL
1. 1st R. E. Mtge.	$ 5,000[a]	$ 3,045[b]	$ 8,045
2. 2d R. E. Mtge.	5,000[c]	3,150[b]	8,150
3. Existing notes and contrs.	8,000[a]	3,255[b]	11,255[a]
4. New Equip. Loan No. 1	12,150[c]	3,402[c]	15,552
5. New Equip. Loan No. 2	1,620[c]	454[c]	2,074
TOTAL	$31,770	$13,306	$45,076

[a]See Chapter 12.
[b]Exhibit 87.
[c]See Chapters 13 and 14.

Exhibit 108

So, if the projection could be made to work at all (i.e., *without* counting on all of the $43,591 of "solutions") there *was* adequate room to meet serial debt payments in the projected year ahead—and it would not be difficult to demonstrate this to the extent necessary.

The *next year?* The requirements climb to $45,076, up $10,970 as the new equipment loans are counted in for a full year: a 32 percent increase.

With the "banker's hat" on, then, going forward it looks as though there is, in the year ahead, enough cash flow to meet serial debt—but also that the needs *increase* the following year, and cash flow—*profits*—will need to go up, too. . . .

But the problem *is:* we are not *asking* the bank to loan *serial* debt (the kind of money related to profit-generation or cash flow). No, we are asking the bank to *participate* in a finance company loan. And, how will a banker look at *that?* Which way, of the "*the* three" ways, do we use to pay off *this* kind of debt?

MORE ACTION

Somewhat puzzled, at this juncture, management called the finance company executive and said it would like to come down and see him the next morning: "I have some questions which I would like to clear up *before* you come out next Monday."

Confronting the commercial finance company officer the next morning, management led off as follows: "As you know, we have been growing—which is why you told me you called on us. Well, we are going to grow a *lot* this next year, and it looks to me as though we might be able to use the services of a company like yours. When you called on me, you mentioned that banks sometimes *participate* in your loans, and you explained how this keeps interest costs down. Now, in recent weeks we have been busy planning for the year ahead—and *if* we decide to do business with your company, or some company like yours, I want our bank—or *a* bank—to participate to the maximum, which as I recall is 50 percent. But what is bothering me a little is *this:* what's in it for the bank? What will prompt the bank to *want* to participate? I've been doing some figuring, and I can see how, with luck, we might need your kind of financing for two, three, or four years . . . ."

The finance company executive responded at length, and in summary made these points:

- Most finance company loans do *not* involve bank participation.
- The principal advantage of *having* bank participation, to the borrower, is a reduction of interest costs.
- It's not the "end of the world" if the bank *doesn't* participate: the finance company won't take a loan for 50% that it wouldn't take at $100%. (Here management recalled its first "solution"—that it would save $4,941 if it got the bank to participate 50%.)
- The reasons banks *do* participate in finance company loans include:
  1. A desire to have in their loan portfolio a secured loan, policed and administered by the finance company.
  2. A desire to stay with a promising customer which has "growing pains," to continue to enjoy its account and to be assured of getting its loan and deposit business again when there is less financial stress, more balances to be left with the bank and its needs are "within bankings' bounds."
- *If* the bank should wish, the finance company *might* be able to provide a "cleanup" for a period of sixty days or so every year or so—even if it is

somewhat artificial—to provide the bank with the "proof of liquidity" its bank examiners often seem to require. "It's been done; that's all I can say."
  • The finance company doesn't *know,* yet, whether it can help or not—"but we'll see you Monday."

Reassured, from this visit, that one way or another, its plans could go forward, management relaxed. It now felt that it would be especially important to share with the banker (*at* the "right" time) its *long*-range thinking: management has dreams of a company with $20,000,000 or more in sales—and clearly the bank would find a piece of this kind of future attractive. . . .

On return to the office, management told the Office Manager of the impending visits from the finance company people and the banker, and instructed him to prepare a "package" of data for each, with "CONFIDENTIAL" to be stamped or written on each document:

For the Bank:
  • Last year's audit report (it has previous ones)
  • Projected P. & L.
  • Projected pro-forma balance sheets

For the Finance Company:
  • Last year's audit report
  • Audit reports, four previous years
  • Projected P. & L.
  • Projected pro-forma balance sheets
  • Collateral calculations (lower portion—lines 6 through 10—of Exhibit 83).
  • Copies of last three accounts receivable agings.
  • Copy of latest accounts payable aging.

THE BANKER'S OUTLOOK

At this point we will leave the "management" of the company we have become so well acquainted with to its own devices, and move on to some more broadly conceived principals and commentary that, hopefully, will be of help to *you,* in arranging the finances of your business.

A traditional, time-tested checklist covering the major points included in a banker's professional outlook consists of the "Five C's of Credit:"

Character
Capacity
Collateral
Conditions
Capital

By exploring each of these points it is possible to anticipate your own "strong" and "weak" spots as they will appear to your banker. (Here the term "banker" includes the officers of the finance company or other lending agency you may be dealing with.)

Character

What is there about you that distinguishes you from others? What are your chief characteristics? What kind of reputation do you have? As to moral and ethical matters, what kind of principles govern your behavior; what sort of record do you have? What kind of impression do you leave with others? How would you (and how do *others*) describe your personality? What about your physical health? Your mental and emotional health? All of these factors—and more—enter into what the banker will be thinking about you as he visits with you, checks with others about you, and ponders your plans.

Along with almost everyone else, remember that your friendly banker may be guilty of oversimplification: it is all too easy for all of us to "tag" or "label" each other. If you *are* "tagged" or "labeled," what does the tag or label mean?

- "Salesman type"
- "A lightweight"
- "A lady's man"
- "Plodding and unimaginative, but honest"
- "A good engineer, but not a manager"
- "A perennial optimist"
- "Probably very able, but lazy"
- "Somehow I feel uneasy around him"
- "A natural leader"
- "A capable manager"
- "Aggressive, but well-organized"
- "High-principled, strongly motivated"
- "Ambitious and very capable"
- "Personable and intelligent"
- "A strong man on any team"
- "Has his feet on the ground"

If, as you take a good look in the mirror, or imagine what others think of you, you *do* come up with some *negative* factors (and if it's a good mirror or an honest inventory of others' views, who will emerge spotless?), what do you *do* about them? It is the mere recognition of weaknesses that represents the first step toward overcoming them. The next step, doing something constructive to balance the scale positively, is often more difficult. It might help to pose this question: suppose *you* were the prospective lender, and you knew these weak points—sensed these areas of vulnerability; what could possibly overcome them? For example, a company president who is a good salesman "but a poor manager" might make it a point to use his sales ability to persuade some people who *are* good managers to join his organization, perhaps even including in their responsibilities the management of *his* efforts.

And, with so much emphasis on forward-planning, it might be well to note that it can be a source of strength to have also at least considered the path of retreat or retrenchment, should that become necessary.

Above all, be yourself: good bankers are among the best judges of people, and any efforts to leave a false impression are not likely to succeed.

Capacity

Does this company have the capacity to pay us back the money we loan to it? Does this man have the ability to manage the business effectively? Does his *organization* have the capacity to function without this man, if necessary? What percentage of plant capacity is being used now; what will it be in the future? Does management have the capacity to grow and develop with its business? Does this company have the capacity to survive and prosper in its industry? Does this customer have the capacity to develop into a more important, more profitable customer? Is this company *legally* organized to carry out its program? Such are the thoughts your banker may have. . . . Be prepared to supply solid answers to these questions, and—wherever possible— to provide the banker with tangible evidence to support your answers.

Collateral

In case the company's plans are not successful, and we must foreclose on our collateral, what will we have—and will we be able to collect our loan from the proceeds? Is our collateral adequately insured? To whom could we sell the collateral? Where will our collateral be located? How often can we get figures and certifications as to the collateral? What does our collateral *look* and *feel* like?—These are the kinds of questions your lender is likely to have concerning collateral; are you ready for them?

The less *capital* you have (the lower your net worth) in relation to your total debt, the more interest a lender will take in your collateral—simply because it is, under circumstances where there is a heavy debt load, more likely that the lender could actually be placed in a position where repayment of the loan would depend on successful liquidation of the collateral.

One thing that you can consider, as a means of improving the collateral position, is offering to assign existing "keyman" life insurance on your life. The company may already have such insurance or agree to obtain and assign it. This will indicate the confidence you have in your program and provide assurance to the lender that, if it decides to go ahead—in part because of a high regard for you—that if you should meet an unexpected death and not be able to follow through as you would if alive, the lender's interests would be protected. This measure may also be wise from your own standpoint, and prudent from an estate-planning vantage point.

Assuming that you are incorporated and that the capital stock of the company is closely held, you can expect the lender to require that you and your associates-in-ownership (and perhaps also their wives) personally guarantee the company's borrowings. These guarantees will be sought—and, wisely, given—as tangible evidence of the fact that you have every confidence in your operation, and that you will "stand behind" the company's transactions. It is important that your bank and/or other lender feel *comfortable* with the collateral package offered, and when loans are predicated on "pieces of paper," like accounts receivable, it is reassuring for a lender to know that the people responsible for the conduct of the business have their *personal* worth and entity involved. This is true, incidentally, *even* if your personal financial statement does not disclose much in the way of net worth, aside from your ownership in the company. Such guarantees tell your banker that if it *should* come to a point of having to realize on the collateral, the man best equipped to achieve such realization (you) will be on deck to attend to that then-vital business.

And, there is something else you can do, as to collateral—again, assuming that your business is incorporated and that you (and perhaps a few associates) own at least a controlling interest in the company. If unexpected troubles are encountered (and it *is* the *un*expected that everyone really has to fear), it is conceivable that in order for the lender's interest to be protected it would be desirable to *sell* your company as a *going* business; that is, by selling stock ownership, rather than directly liquidating the collateral. Although this step should not be lightly undertaken, if you are really "betting your future" and are required or deem it necessary or desirable to do so, you can "put your money where your mouth is" and pledge to the lender, to support your personal guaranty, all of the capital stock that you and/or your associates own in your company. This rather drastic move puts your bank, finance company, or other lender in a more flexible position, and—particularly if you have a business with a really attractive sales-potential—should make the collateral position of the lender more comfortable. And, if you should decide to play this "ace-in-the-hole" certainly no one can thereafter question your commitment to your future plans.

Conditions

"Conditions," said one old credit hand, "are what change—for the worse— *after* you extend the credit." If so, it is about *conditions* that a lender is especially concerned.

What is the condition—what are the trends—of the overall economy? To what extent are these same conditions true for our area, and for the areas served by this business? What is the outlook for the industry of which this business is a part? The outlook for the industries served by this business? What represents the competition for this business; and how are those companies faring? What is the situation as regards labor relations in this industry? When does this company's union contract expire, and what is the outlook? Are there any special legal conditions affecting this company? Is this company "riding" or "bucking" trends? Any special zoning, licensing, or pollution problems? What are marketing trends? What key economic indicators tie in with this business? What industry association does this company belong to; does it issue comparative statistics? What is the *total* market for this company's products, and what percentage of the total market does this company enjoy? If conditions should change significantly, is the management of this company prepared to "trim its sails" accordingly?

Your banker is going to be pretty well informed regarding national, regional, and local economic conditions. But he may need some help in understanding the basic elements and conditions affecting your own industry: be prepared to produce appropriate data to assist him in comprehending your particular industry's—and company's—position.

Capital

Your assets, less your liabilities, equal your net worth—and the net worth of your company *is* the net wealth employed in your business, or your capital. If you have *enough* of it, you don't need to borrow money; instead, you are looking for new ways to invest it. The *less* of it you have, the smaller your capital in relation to the scope of your business and the amounts you need to borrow, the riskier it is for a lender to work with you.

Frequently, in a closely held company, debt arises due to officers and/or owners of the company. Such debt may arise from the nonpayment of accrued salaries or bonuses, or may represent the after-tax portion of bonuses loaned back to the company, or new outside funds loaned to the business. In any event, the "capital" of the business may be enhanced, as far as a lender is concerned, if such funds are "frozen in." Legally, this is accomplished by "subrogating" or "subordinating" the debt insofar as the bank or other lender is concerned. That is, by the creditor and the company both formally agreeing that the debt will not be repaid as long as the company is in debt to the bank, or at least, not without the bank's formal, written permission.

To illustrate the effect of such subordinations, let's look at the balance sheet of the company we have studied in detail as part of this projection effort. Specifically, looking ahead to December of the year ahead, we find (Exhibit 84, p. 128).

Total liabilities	$468,711
Net worth	$100,750

The "debt to worth" ratio, then, would be 4.65 to 1 ($468,711 divided by $100,750). But, what if management agreed to *subordinate* the $16,700 owing to it ("Due to Officers")? What does this do to the ratio?

Total liabilities	$468,711
Less "due to officers"	(16,700)
Adjusted T. L.	$452,011
Net worth	$100,750
Plus "due to officers"	16,700
Adjusted N. W.	$117,450

The new "Debt to Worth" ratio: 3.93 to 1 ($452,011 divided by $117,450). It is interesting to compare this with "last year's" ratio: 3.50 to 1 (see Exhibit 5, p. 22).

Then, too, it is of course possible to create *other* kinds of subordinated debt; remember when the sale of debentures was considered? Such debt is normally subordinated to institutional lenders.

It is appropriate, when discussing "capital" with your banker, to be aware of the net overall earnings you expect to make on your net worth:

Net worth—End of last year	$ 72,900
Net worth—Dec. of proj. year	100,750
TOTAL	$173,650

A. Average net worth (T. div. by 2)	$ 86,825
B. Estimated earnings (Ex. 65)	$ 27,850
C. "Earnings on net worth" (B div. by A)	32.7%

This compares to 38.9 percent for last year (Exhibit 10, p. 26). In one sense, this ratio is high because the company is "highly leveraged" (with debt), or—to put it another way—undercapitalized. On the other hand, this key ratio tells management that it is going to be *building* capital at a healthy rate. And you should be ready to point out *your* "earnings on net worth" picture to your prospective lenders.

17
A Parting Word

The Soviet command-style economy, with its rigid planning, central controls and bias against experimentation, simply no longer works effectively. Specialization demands decentralization. No single, central planning agency can fine-tune a diversified modern economy. The industrialized world has passed into a new and more mature technological stage in which, as Wayne State Professor Richard Burks puts it, "Economic growth will depend on releasing the creative energies of an ever more numerous intelligentsia, and on the granting of wide-ranging autonomy to enterprises functioning in a market situation." . . . In this new stage, individual creativity and enterprise are essential.

—Pages 30–35, *Time* magazine,
March 29, 1971

THE END OF A JOURNEY

IT HAS BEEN A LONG AND, HOPEFULLY, INTERESTING TRIP: WE HAVE "looked over its shoulder" as the management of a specific business has, first, examined its past (as reflected in financial statements), reviewed carefully its present position, and then gone ahead to develop and define its future plans. As we have looked, we have had an opportunity to absorb something of the approaches and techniques utilized in organizing the information that describes the company's future plans. And, we have seen how the company's financial requirements emerged from the projection, and how management plans to meet these needs. Finally, we have seen how management plans to use its projection experience to control actual performance in the future and, in the last chapter, we have reviewed some of the credit principles that bankers and other lenders use in reaching their decisions.

A management that has gone through a process akin to all this is bound to be in a better position than it would otherwise be to arrange for its financial requirements. Also, as a by-product of the effort it should have a better grasp than ever before of all the various aspects of its operations, and be better equipped to direct and monitor the actual operation of its business in the future.

YOU AND THE FUTURE

You have an interest in profits, or you would not have been attracted initially to this book, to say nothing of reaching this point in it. And, if you did not already fully appreciate the necessity of influencing bankers, as well as knowing something about *how to go about* influencing them, you should by now. The projection effort presented in this book is based on actual experience encountered in hundreds of different real-life situations, and one hallmark of management talent is the ability to learn from such "artificial" or shared experience, rather than having to learn everything "the hard way."

So ideally, you have already benefited from your reading. But the real test of the value of the time you have devoted to this book is likely to come when you begin to "marry" your newly acquired outlooks and knowledge to specific elements in your own situation. In this connection, depending on your own background you might— looking back over this projection effort—feel that any comparably sized company that had followed the processes described here would have established along the way a very good system for running its business. And, up to a point, this is true. But it would be unfair and dishonest not to warn you of the limitations and warnings that should go along with such a conclusion. No, what you have experienced here is really just a *beginning*. Sound, it is—because it is based on good, solid principles ("study the past," "move from the known to the unknown," "management by exception," "leave good tracks")—and utilizes proven and time-tested approaches. But the level of management skills reflected here is *not* adequate for every situation, nor for all time.

Assuming that you have arrived at the same point reached by management in our case-study company, you will soon find yourself responding to new problems and challenges. You will probably find that solutions to some of your future problems depend upon your developing capabilities (for yourself *and* within your organization) with regard to matters such as these:

- Cost accounting systems
- Production planning
- Government regulations
- Data processing
- Organization charts
- Job descriptions
- Union negotiations

- New product introduction
- Market analysis
- Employee job safety
- Quality control systems
- Term loan financing
- Public stock issues
- Automated machinery
- Pension funds
- Stock options
- Antipollution measures
- Pricing policy
- Mergers, acquisitions

To meet these future challenges you will need to continue growing, with your business. Bring to these problems the same interest, zest, and industry which have brought you this far in exploring the projection process via this book, and you will find that you can *build* on the abilities you have acquired. Perhaps the principal advantage of the projection approach is its comprehensive, all-encompassing nature: *all* business problems are ultimately described in accounting terms and have financial implications. Therefore, your projection know-how will serve you well in the future, as you dig deep into other types of business problems, and then, in the end, seek to relate them to the overall operation—as required in the projection process.

Every week in the United States alone there are thousands of new incorporations, as new businesses enter our economy—and hundreds of business failures. Many of the failures could have been success stories if the businesses had employed better financial planning. And those of the new businesses that move ahead and develop into successful operations will do so, in part, because their management utilizes sound financial projecting practices.

Good luck, as you set out to "win profits" and "influence bankers" for your own enterprise!

Index